The Eternal Moment

Seeking Divine Presence in the Present

John R. Harris, Ph.D.

The Eternal Moment
John R. Harris

Copyright © John R. Harris 2020
Rome, Georgia

Cover photos and design by John Harris.

For Owen...

Thanks for the late-evening phone conversations:
they planted the seeds of what follows.

Other Books by John R. Harris Published Through Amazon Kindle

Educational:
The Traditional Mind in Greco-Roman Antiquity and Ancient Ireland (essays)
An Introductory Course in Greek and Latin Grammar and Vocabulary
(textbook)
Three Medieval Celtic Renditions of an Ancient Indo-European Myth
(translations)

Non-Fiction:
Climbing Backward Out of Caves (Christian apologetics)
Literary Decline and the Death of the Soul (literary criticism/philosophy)
We Even Saw Figures Tending Fires (faith/philosophy)
Nightmare Made of Dreams (political philosophy)

Baseball
Hitting Secrets From Baseball's Graveyard (history/instruction)
Landing Safeties (instruction)
Key to a Cold City (history)
Metal Ropes (instruction)

Fiction:
El Moreno, Vendetta Di Dio (novel)
Eventually, It All Gets Used (poetry)
A Sleepless Man Might Earn Two Wages (short stories)
Worse by Seven (novel)
Ivory Gutter Shining Bright (short stories)
Footprints in the Snow of the Moon (novel)

CONTENTS

PART ONE

Crosscurrents Bending Our Earthly Timeline

CHAPTER ONE

The Present: Focal Point or Vanishing Point?

Tha tím am fiadh an Coille Hallaig.

Time is the deer in Hallaig Forest.
Gaelic proverb

I really don't know what the proverb from the Isle of Skye—which I found cited by Gaelic poet Sorley MacLean in an anthology—is supposed to mean. I doubt, frankly, that it's a genuine proverb at all. MacLean places it in quotation marks without any attribution, so I concluded that it was some saying of ancient provenance... but it doesn't have the proper ring. Utterances that reach us through a process of lengthy oral transmission are rarely cryptic in the manner of this one. The average fisherman or crofter is far too practical, too down-to-earth, to impose a deer's form upon something as abstract as time. What are we being invited to think here, after all? Is it simply that time bolts away (*tempus fugit*) and can't be caught, so that you're forever running after it—running short of it—in this life? Or is there something mythical behind the saying: is time the White Stag of medieval romance, for instance, that lures so many Arthurian knights into otherworldly adventures? And why would it be that? Because we never know what the future holds—because each new day is a potential adventure of the most exotic sort?

In my old age, I find more and more that the terms I used to accept in thinking about time have grown cliché. For that matter, as far as my age, I'm not officially old by the standard introduced in the Sphinx's riddle to Oedipus: I'm still walking on two legs without the aid of a cane. Like that ancient riddle, a dozen other customary analogies invite us to portion time up into a triad: the past, the present, and the future. The past, they say (we say—everyone but me, I guess), is over and done with. You can't do anything with or to it now: its book is closed. The future is another book, whose cover you haven't yet opened. Who knows what words we may read upon its pages? They could be... well, what could they *not* be? The human imagination poses the only limit to them.

That leaves the present. Here we are, neither wandering back into a past that can't be changed nor straying into a future not sufficiently material to be shaped. Our only genuine reality exists here, exists now. Why do we waste so much energy grieving over past deeds that can never be undone, or fantasizing about future deeds that we cannot yet begin to execute? Why don't we just concentrate upon the part of life directly in front of us: the present? If we would infuse our thoughts and our actions into the here-and-now, we would discover our best chance of finding true happiness. The folly of trying to re-live moments already lived or of trying to live moments whose birth is months or years away would be filtered from our mortal struggle, and we could take our satisfaction in simply *being*.

The previous paragraph has somewhat clumsily summarized (all summaries are somewhat clumsy) a stunningly successful book by Eckhart Tolle titled *The Power of Now*. I was introduced to the little volume by an enthusiastic reader who himself had learned of it through popular culture. I confess that I was disappointed after the build-up; in some ways, I even grew a bit annoyed with what I read. Not that Mr. Tolle would approve all the inferences that I have divined in the shadows of his discussion... but I do not believe they are *faulty* inferences. I suspect he may not have thought through certain angles with the kind of skepticism (and perhaps cynicism) that life has bestowed upon my methods of analysis. His spirit is probably gentler than mine.

Let's start with the past. It isn't really over and done with at all, unless you're incapable of learning or have a haughty contempt for your ancestors' cumulative experience. We should not only allow the past (both our own trial-and-error education and the acquired wisdom of our predecessors) to teach us in the present; we should also display appropriate, constructive regret today for our personal blunders yesterday. We should take responsibility. We should have a conscience.

And then the future. To regard tomorrow as a thrilling fantasy that might potentially feature time-traveling shape-shifters riding unicorns through stargates is to manifest the intellect of a five-year-old child. Mr. Tolle is entirely correct to warn us away from such childish imbecility... but that isn't the proper way to think about the future, in the first place. No sane adult disjoins the terms of tomorrow utterly from those of today. We know, rather, that the former will be heavily conditioned by the latter. What we do just now is not just for now; it is, rather, for tomorrow—and the next day, and the next day.

Indeed, one might well say that the present is the *least real* of these three highly poeticized chronological elements. There's really no such thing as an independent "now". The immediate present is forever fleeting, and also forever forming. Only a lower animal would do something at this instant without any reference at all to what it had done a minute ago and without a thought to what it would be doing a minute from now. A human mind would operate at such a level only in the first stages of infancy or in an advanced stage of impairment. There can be no absolutely, exclusively *now* sort of "now" for a waking creature possessing some measure of free will.

Could it be that the book in question was so spectacularly successful because we of this historical moment are uniquely tormented by things both past and future? Memories of less-than-stellar behavior follow us around like a bad odor. Our society lures and prods us to sate shallow appetites of all kinds instantly. We live to please our senses... which brings us many a proverbial "morning after" full of regret and guilt. That's not all the next day brings, however. In the mail arrive bills to be paid after our fits of pleasure-seeking. We need a job, a salary. Our ancestors often secured an income by working in family businesses, or at least going into stable trades deeply embedded in local communities. We no longer inhabit that kind of world. The jobs of our grandparents (or even our parents) have been absorbed by mechanization or shipped overseas, and what few new jobs blossom require costly training in previously unheard-of skills.

So the past is a repository of empty bottles, crumpled receipts, and useless advice from well-meaning but clueless relatives; and the future is a chaotic merry-go-round of Siren-like temptresses who offer no security in their promises of constant novelty. Maybe we're fleeing into the present moment and gathering ourselves into the fetal position the way a soldier in the heat of battle jumps into a foxhole and hugs himself as shells explode all around.

Suicide rates are surging—an inexplicable trend in a society that prides itself on its facility for making "progress" (whatever that is). The recreational use of depressants, as well, points to our need for "micro-suicides" on an almost daily basis. This, I suspect—I fear—is how we go about "living in the present" most of the time. That is, we lock the doors and bar the windows against past and future for a blessed hour or so of nullity when we can. The very absence of past and future, artificially engineered, is our adored present.

I alluded to the Sirens of Homer's *Odyssey* just above. Their shore is littered with the bones of sailors who have heard their enchanting song, leapt overboard in oblivion to their journey's purpose, and swum to a nameless beach where they waste away. Earlier during the same ill-starred voyage, the eaters of the lotus had past and future similarly erased from their minds. Destiny seems less grim in that adventure, but only because the lotus-eaters linger like specters in an eternal lack of orientation rather than giving up the ghost and rotting away.

I well know that such refugees from life who have retreated to limbo are not exemplars of Mr. Tolle's "power of now". Nevertheless, I worry that they represent only too accurately the way most of us cultivate an attention to the present moment. What we find in the "now" cannot be mere absence of the "then" if it is to be spiritually rewarding. On the contrary, I would insist that in the past lies the secret to understanding the present in all its supernatural amplitude.

CHAPTER TWO

The Past: Not as Buried as You Think

Oú sont-ils, Vierge Souvereine…
Mais oú sont les neiges d'antan?

Where are they [the great women of the past], Blessed Virgin…
Well, where are the snows of yesteryear?
François Villon

In the foregoing chapter, I defended the past as a repository of important lessons about how to navigate the present. That, I'm afraid, is another cliché—and, as still another cliché runs, there's an element of truth to every cliché. The implication in such half-profound almost-wisdom is that clichés also contain large doses of falsehood. In this instance, treating the past as nothing but a box of tips about exploiting advantages in the present shortchanges our yesterdays woefully. Is the value of things past, then, only in their slipping us a trump card to win the hand we're playing right now? Is that all that matters—the "right now"?

The Greek philosopher Epicurus is credited (or discredited) with having enunciated a hedonist value system: one, that is, where the highest objective in life is pleasure. The attribution is careless, in that what Epicurus truly placed at the apex of the value pyramid was freedom from pain—not quite the same thing. Pleasure is of value in this view to the extent that it relieves pain. Among the premier analgesics (literally, "pain-relievers") proposed by the philosopher was the recollection of past pleasures. In a moment of extreme distress, a sufferer can dredge up an especially happy time from memory and ride out the waves with greater tranquility.

I don't really care for that "defense" of the past's merits, either… but it's getting closer to Ground Zero. My objection is that Epicurus reduces the past to an alternate reality capable of bringing the sun back out on a rainy day—a fraudulent alternative, since what happened yesterday is not in fact happening today, and the wide gap between the two is indeed precisely why recalling yesterday is recommended. Use of the past to create such willful self-delusion bestows little honor upon our memories. On the contrary, it turns the past into a fifth of Scotch whiskey or a joint of marijuana. In Epicurus, we remember things that we found enjoyable to escape from things that we find intensely unenjoyable. Since my argument will be that the past is indeed a window upon a higher reality, the proposition here that its best use is escapist doesn't much appeal to me.

For some of the most powerful moments of the past—some of those we preserve with deepest reverence—aren't very pleasurable in any obvious sense: they draw nothing from any comfortable sensation centered upon our flattered ego or satisfied hunger. The fifteenth-century poet Villon was brooding over all the radiant, magnificent women of the past no longer on this earth when he asked in the banner citation above, "Where are the snows of yesteryear?" A century later, his countryman Joachim Du Bellay penned some masterful sonnets conceived when, while touring Italy, he found himself amid the dilapidated relics of ancient Rome. A little more than two centuries farther along the linear road that organizes our understanding the past, Romantic poets and artists throughout Western Europe were poking among ruined villages, listening to the wind whistle through empty castles, and gazing over ragged moors once prowled by Celtic warriors or Homeric heroes. The past had become a very distinct and powerful transmitter of *painful* recollections... and yet, in that pain of a gilded age lost forever nestled the strangest of pleasures. Philosophers of the time called it *the sublime*.

Or they would have, if they had extended sublimity to time as well as space. In his *Critique of Judgment*, Immanuel Kant described the sublime as contrastive with the beautiful. Beauty is apprehended without any disruptive movement of the eyes; the sublime phenomenon cannot be taken in at a glance, or even by a mere sweep of the gaze. The beautiful object is limited and balanced; the sublime experience scarcely even represents a discernible object, so titanic and restless are its contours. Vast seascapes, glowering cloudbanks, abysmal mountain crevasses or peaks rising from cliff upon cliff... such scenes as these operate in two ways upon the human perceiver. First, they impress upon him the utter insignificance of his bodily reality (but not so as to inspire immediate terror: if lightning were flying from a nearby cloudbank or an avalanche falling from a peak just overhead, the meditative nature of the encounter would be shattered). Upon the heels of this sense of puniness, however, arises an awareness of oneself as a spiritual being: a soul mightily liberated from the body to measure its soaring range against nature's most stupendously huge displays. In such competition, the human soul always wins—for its magnitude exceeds even Everest's, scaling all the way up to God's throne.

In these ideas, we see the origin of Byron's Childe Harold, of Chateaubriand's René, of Caspar David Friedrich's inimitable canvases where lonely wanderers stare into alpine chasms... and surely of Beethoven's symphonies, their orchestra multiplied to generate unprecedented volumes of crashing sound in irresistible climax. By the early nineteenth century, the notion that Man (with a capital "m") rises to God's feet in all his various incarnations as peasant, sailor, vagrant, orphan—the notion of the Rights of Man explicit in the American Declaration of Independence—had been launched from a profound spiritual rebirth.

Its trajectory, alas, did not always carry to heaven. Sometimes, as we shall see, the yawning crevasse that elicited such triumph over material circumstance also became the material destination of a delirious excess.

I haven't forgotten about the "sepulchral" poetry of my earlier examples, which hardly seems to be measuring the Alps. (Italian poet Ugo Foscolo actually titled his collection *I Sepolchri*.) Remember Hamlet lingering over Yorick's remains as the gravedigger hands him the old jester's skull? At the scene's end, the moody prince utters the verses, "Imperial Caesar, dead and turned to clay, / Might stop a hole to keep the wind away." What has that perspective in common with gazing up at the Milky Way? Quite a lot, I think. Though I've never heard this vein of literature classed as sublime, it strikes me as straining *chronological* limits just as the seascape or the a vast ice floe from a Friedrich painting battles against spatial limits. The mind, first of all, must accept a very humbling estimate of the body it inhabits... as if to say, "You puny man! So you thought you would do great things, write great books. The names of explorers, inventors, conquerors, poets, and composers far greater than you are no longer even legible on their gravestones!" Yet such humility is at once succeeded by a spiritual transcendence of individual identity and a fusion (or something in the vicinity) with a divine perspective. Suddenly this puny human can view the vast, pathetic bombast and futility of all human endeavor throughout history almost with the eye of God.

The prospect of the past, you see, can elevate us right out of our pitiful worldly selves. Of what other experience are we capable which can so suppress that all-but-indomitable egotism within us?

Yet I also suspect that the "chronological sublime" is a particular source of the immense danger I mentioned above in passing, and to which I will return. At about the same historical moment as Romantic artists were staring vacantly down the slope of things long done and long forgotten, they (or their brethren engaged in other revolutions of thought) were also beginning to stare down the far slope—the slope of the future, seen from this new vantage. Of that, more anon.

What I want finally to say of the past before concluding this chapter is that even the ethereal vistas of the sublime do not exhaust the spiritual wealth of our memory's treasures. In fact, the prospects that most effectively nudge us out of our dull transit through linear time may be those opening right at our feet rather than in the stars or where sea meets sky. They may or may not involve visual panoramas, may or may not convey something whose terms are unique in our experience. Forgive me if I elucidate by offering five brief examples from my own life. It's the only life I know intimately: I'm sure that your time in this world offers many cases of a similar sort.

In *The Wanderer*, Caspar David Friedrich captures the psychological effect of a sublime moment. The faces of his lonely figures (and he represents many in contemplative scenes like this one) are never fully visible. I think that's because the vast, abysmal vistas unfurled at their feet or before their lifted gaze are the true portrait of their soul, beside which a flesh-and-blood face would reveal only superficial truth.

CHAPTER THREE

Memories Ever Present: "The Divine Bides Here"

Rivedo i luoghi dove un giorno ho pianto:
Un sorriso mi sembra ora quel pianto.

I see again those places where tears once stung my eyes,
Distance makes their weeping wear into a smile.
Giovani Pascoli

Here, then, are several instances of memories from the course of my own life that refuse to relinquish their hold upon me, even though most have nothing about them that would interest a great artist.

I couldn't have been more than three or four years old. My sister was scarcely walking on her own. The two of us were playing in a back yard that seemed as big as half the world to us, but was actually attached to a clapboard house of well under a thousand square feet. My mother was standing close by. A bright red cardinal began singing, and Mom uttered some word or other of delight that drew my attention to her. She was a complicated person, my mother. Her moments of happiness, such as they were, often came purloined from circumstances that she had twisted around to her liking. She didn't take a lot of pleasure in human relationships. Sometimes, fortunately, she was able to find direct, spontaneous joy in simpler things. She loved birds; and at that instant, though a mere toddler, I could tell that she was sincerely enchanted by the cardinal's lilts. (By the way, cardinals used to sing a much fuller song many decades ago. An arrogant wag mocked me lately for affirming as much, as if I were giving free rein to an idiotic burst of nostalgia; but I know what I heard—and I haven't heard that ampler song in any Southern or Western state for half a century.)

In the same back yard some two or three years later, possibly standing in the same precise spot, I was amusing myself all alone with a plastic red-and-white propeller plane that was my pride and joy at the time. I believe I was wearing Sunday clothes, or was otherwise dressed with unusual care; perhaps it was Easter Sunday. The adults were all attending to other business at the moment, and I was free to play any game whose imaginary terms didn't require my knees to touch the grass. Stretching my arm as far as it would reach, I chose to pilot my craft high into an utterly clear mid-morning zenith—cerulean-blue, and ringing with sunlight like a bronze dome. At just that instant, I heard an actual plane's propeller snoring invisibly in the fathomless sky. It transfixed me, that sound. It drew me up to the bronzed blue edge of the stratosphere, and I stood wondering... wondering something like, "Just how big is the universe?"

One more moment from the old home's back yard (a humble place we would leave behind forever in upward mobility when I was ten): now I was alone, once again, in a treehouse that my father, the engineer, had cleverly constructed for us children. A morning hour this time, too... strange, how my magical recollections on that property congregate around mornings. Again, as well, the vegetation was distinctly green, meaning that the season must have been more spring than summer, when grass would go brown in our North Texas neighborhood. In fact, the air was crisp, and I was wearing a coat whose collar hugged my neck. Was this our final year in the tiny house—had I already taken my first glimpses at the elite school where other children would be telling me, "You don't belong here," for the next several years? Or did that come later? Maybe I was suffering through my first crush... in third grade, on a girl from Canada named Gloria Cross who might have been the princess of Ireland's "Snow White" legend. (A raven spilling a carcass's blood in fresh snow once made a wistful prince imagine the perfect woman's hair and lips and skin; the next day he left home to search the wide world for her.)

For some reason—and probably for neither of the foregoing—I sensed an acute pain as I peered across our neighbor's yard, across the rural highway beyond that, across the railroad tracks and the broad meadow to a line of trees a mile or two away. I felt... that life was immeasurably more than I understood, and that it all lay before me, and that... that I wasn't going to be able to catch up with its receding horizon. Though I wouldn't encounter the German word *Sehnsucht* (literally, "reaching as far as the eye can see") for at least two more decades, I fully understood its definition from that day forward.

A final childhood memory (by no means the last, but the last I shall relate here) is really an aggregate of similar experiences repeated year after year. Every Thanksgiving, we would pile into my father's '53 Chevy wagon and wind down two-lane highways (starting with the one I could see from the treehouse) to my grandparents' in Austin. The

Interstate was not yet completely constructed, and the trip consumed almost four hours, as I recall. We children would doze for much of the way; but by the time we neared Austin, all three of us would be wide awake to see who could be first to spot the Capitol's dome—which, believe it or not, was visible from a good ten or twelve miles off in those days.

The moment that leaps out oddly from the ensuing succession of events, however, has nothing triumphal or palatial about it. A sense of eerie mystery, rather, would descend upon me as we rolled along utterly empty, pallidly streetlit avenues to the corner of Fourteenth and San Antonio. Whether it was some early incarnation of Breckinridge Hospital or another multi-storied structure that we passed, the particular image of a flat façade and bleak windows won't release my mind. Why not—why the persistence of this Gothic gloom? My grandmother was the most angelic person on earth to me, and she was now minutes away. Perhaps, indeed, the magic lay therein, just as a Christmas tree's lights cast no spell without layers of shadowy pine needles gathered around them. Like a benign supernatural figure in a fairy tale, my grandmother could be reached only after hours of thickening darkness and foreign, deathly empty habitations. And the deathliest of these last has never departed my imagination.

Just to prove that not all such mystical instants, suspended forever from linear time, were not restricted to childhood, I may briefly add that I logged several such moments when walking through the British Isles on three different occasions in my twenties. The most spectacular of these was a protracted moment—perhaps consuming half an hour while my inner clock remained frozen—as I wound up a Scots glen. I had started the day in Edinburgh, crossed the Firth of Forth Bridge, made my way through Dunfermline by mid-afternoon, and was now (over twenty-five miles into the hike) wondering why I hadn't called it a day before leaving that city behind. I could see for four or five miles in every direction (maybe more: Highlanders say to take your best estimate of distance in this terrain and double it). I saw no sign that a bed-and-breakfast might magically appear in some fold of the vast landscape (though one would do so not too much farther along). The season was mid-summer, so I would have daylight or dusk to guide me until about eleven o'clock at night... which, somehow, wasn't a great comfort. Nothing detectable to my senses indicated that a single shoe, or foot, or tire, or hoof, or paw stirred anywhere along the road behind or ahead of me, or up the glen's gigantic far shoulder that paralleled my crawl from five miles away (call it ten). I could willingly enough have laid myself down to sleep in my tracks—or to die.

Yet when I noticed the low sunlight slanting through an inaudible rain shower down at the glen's base, and then watched that same sunlight fan out ever more generously as my eyes lifted to the road ahead, I couldn't imagine any place on earth where I would rather give myself to an eternal sleep.

I could hardly describe a more sublime experience, following Professor Kant's text to the letter, if I were deliberately to make something up; so allow me to add one more moment of a less Romantic caliber. I don't believe it occurred on the same tour, and my physical state was not remotely so near to exhaustion. I simply paused atop an elevation more or less in the dead center of Ireland, somewhere around the town of Tullamore (which happens to mean "big hill"—perhaps this very place was the eponymous rise). From there, as an unencumbered midday sun beat down upon the most fertile grazing and farmland the human eye has ever seen, I had the sense of the land's practically sweating golden heat back up into the clear sky. I could hear cows moo distantly. I could feel human civilization fast asleep, comfortably plunged into a living sleep, amid the natural cradle where it had made minimal adjustments. I didn't even have to turn my head from north to south or lift my gaze to any horizon. It was just there, at my feet: peace. Peace on earth.

Now that my Tullamore recollection has filtered through as 5b, I seem to have ended up with a pool of six past experiences that will linger in my mind, I'm sure, as long as I draw breath. And maybe, after my last breath, they will cease lingering and come back to full life—or fully reveal the life within them whose echo I could but faintly detect while in this world.

Was any of the six a "delight", of the kind that Epicurus recommended in carefully preserved memories? I suppose my mother's rare moment of genuine happiness might be of such a nature... but not really; for essential to its character is my awareness (perhaps already kindling in me as a toddler) that she had few such moments. In that joy was pathos. You could say that my grand overview of the Scots glen was delightful... except that I was half dead at the time, or at least feeling myself to be so. Let us not quibble over a word. All I mean to emphasize here is that these were not moments of toasting the health of jolly good fellows, celebrating conference championships with teammates, high-fiving close friends after landing a new job...

nothing festive. Not even remotely. Maybe Epicurus, so maligned for being an Epicure, didn't intend for fanfare to characterize the pleasant past. In any case, it's not a distinguishing quality of my personal samples.

One might charge that my attempt to separate these half-dozen experiences from the artistic sublime of the previous chapter breaks down as early as the treehouse, or even the toy airplane—and that the Highland glen or the Tullamore hill would indeed have made Casper David Friedrich send for his easel. What I've tried to get across, though, is that my moments had no sequence of reflections leading from physical puniness to spiritual transcendence. Their impression was instant. It was "just there". It liberated me from the sense of linear time so effectively that I might almost have been convinced of having lost consciousness briefly. Does great art do the same thing, drawing us out of time in the same way? I would certainly agree that it does; but art is *artifice*: it owes its existence to the mediation of a gifted mind that alters the world's routine terms for us. These experiences were *immediate* in the word's root sense. They actually belonged to reality's routine—though for most of us, most of the time, they turn out to be hidden within our mind's dull distillation of that routine.

And here I may advance a remark that perhaps goes to the heart of the matter. Why was it so much easier for me to find examples of the "non-linear, abiding moment" in my childhood recollections than in my adult ones? The answer must surely be that, as we mature, we grow more conditioned by our cultural environment. We filter out data of lesser relevance to critical decisions involving physical safety and material success. There's nothing particularly sordid or degenerate about this process. Romantics of all stripes (but especially academics) like to fault cultural conditioning with making us less sensitive and spiritual beings. The truth is that, if we carried our child's wonder at new things away with us to a busy college campus at the ripe age of eighteen, we'd probably be mugged, run over, and arrested for vagrancy all within a week. In a pre-capitalist society, we would merely be mauled by a cougar and bitten by a rattlesnake. The diminishing sensitivity of our spiritual receptors as we age conceals nothing sinister. It's somewhat responsible, rather, for our success at aging.

Nevertheless, there's a regrettable absence of spiritual moments in our adult routine: we can probably agree upon that. I was no doubt more susceptible to the "numinous moment" during my ambulatory vacations abroad precisely because I had wrenched myself out of my familiar setting. The Latin phrase, *numen inest*—"something divine bides here"—was a quasi-ritual utterance that an ancient might utter upon blundering into such an occasion as I have been describing. Living closer to nature, peoples of simpler times probably had more such encounters. Our more progressive societies in the West used to carve out a weekly place in the urban/suburban grind for what one might call "salutary dislocation". That place was Sunday church. Our forefathers would enter shadowy, strangely resonant buildings that looked nothing like their workplace or residence. There they would free their minds to "cast a pale eye on life, on death" (as John Donne would write after getting religion) and hear hymns that borrowed more than a little from the sounds of wind stirring tree boughs or of mountainous cliffs echoing a stone's tumble. They would attempt to recover, if only for an hour, something of the child's wonder; for the Master has said that you will not enter the kingdom of Heaven unless you become as a child.

These days, when we go to church at all, the services are often much more "contemporary". We're still seeking the spiritual—perhaps more frantically then ever, since we appear to have less of it than ever—but we wrongly suppose that we will find easier access to it if it can be rendered in terms grown familiar to us. We desire not that the numinous be dislocated from our routine, but that it be infused seamlessly into that routine. Expressions of faith crop up brightly on bumper stickers. An adjustment of lyrics in Rap or Country/Western music makes it "Christian".

Well... to each according to his taste. My objective in the last two chapters, however, has been to argue for a certain apparent "irrelevance" in the spiritual moment. The seams around it are so unfashionably visible that we are apt to pack it away as a "statistical outlier". It contributes nothing to our daily struggle to advance from A to F. It is a flower along the roadside that the mowers somehow managed to miss; it is a child playing quietly in the lounge outside the boardroom because one of the directors couldn't find a baby-sitter. It breaks loose and drifts free, that moment. It trails no coupling that catches and closes upon anything else. It's "just there".

And it belongs to the past as we search for it in our minds because, most often, we notice it only after we have proceeded farther along our linear road to "accomplishment". Then, for no discernible reason at all, it floats to the surface. Dozing off that night, we remember the flower at the roadside or the girl playing under the chair legs. Of all the stupid things to remember… what's *that* doing there?

I will say no more about Eckhart Tolle for the rest of my book's discussion; but, as far as I can make out, this is pretty nearly the kind of moment he has in mind for his *now*. My endeavor over the past few pages has been to suggest that the numinous is indeed "now"—but that it was "now" when it happened, and will be "now" fifty years from today. Its position on our timeline of forward progress doesn't determine its character. That position is what's irrelevant, in the spirit's understanding of relevance.

CHAPTER FOUR

A Brief History of the Future

Not many of us realize, I think, that our habit of looking to the future for better and brighter things is a predisposition characteristic of few human cultures ever to exist: probably a small fraction of one percent. Here I go again with a timeline—and this in an argument against our fixation with timelines! I shall obviously have to repeat, now and often hereafter, that arranging events in a chronological cause-and-effect sequence is hardwired into the human intelligence, even though it may grossly oversimplify the true nature of reality. We cannot process occurrences in any other way, generally speaking. Yet our own highly scientific/technological culture carries the tendency beyond the boundaries of necessity.

We know, for instance, that pre-literate cultures, for which mythology provided answers to what we consider scientific questions, viewed the future almost with contempt, and certainly with uninterest. "What has been is what will be," preaches Ecclesiastes (in a text orally transmitted long before it was written down). "There's nothing new under the sun." Polytheistic traditions are, if anything, even more of a closed historical circle than the Hebraic one. Systems with multiple gods in their heaven tend to represent the world's formative events (when cosmic forces rage against each other) as settling into a heroic age... after which profound novelty grows impossible. In those gilded times of yore, gods and men kept company, feasted together, even selected mates from across the "mortality line"; and when death came to the latter or to the demigods of mixed marriages (for the divine gene seems to be recessive in all mythic traditions), the gods themselves grieved. Sometimes they magically elevated the deceased to sit among them in eternal Olympian corridors.

The Greek poet Hesiod left an epic poem wherein the ensuing process of decline (the so-called Five Ages of Man in *Works and Days*) is detailed. Each later generation of mortals is distinctly punier and more corrupt. Eventually, all of creation appears to topple down in catastrophic destruction, like our theory of the Collapsing Universe—and another Big Bang may set the pendulum swinging again, for that matter (as in the Hindu system or the Scandinavian Ragnarok's aftermath). Except for such an initial creative burst, everything is always spiraling downward. Entropy is the law—a moral entropy that nudges the heroic generation farther and farther into the past. Even our great-grandfathers (if we are products of the tribal mind) were no longer addressing the gods directly. As for us decadents today, we scarcely hold anything in regard beyond our selfish interests. We break formal agreements, strike fraudulent deals, disrespect our elders, and engage in strife over meaningless matters. What future could await such a brood of vipers as we are? Tomorrow can bring only more of the same, and a little bit of something worse.

I doubt that such cultural pessimism prevented tribal peoples from shifting their villages to higher ground, say, when a flooding river swept away existing structures for the third or fourth time. I'm sure they learned to make adjustments, just as we do, designed to secure a better tomorrow. Likewise, we know that certain human beings in recorded time have always wanted too much from the future (and will continue to do so, we must believe). We know this because the Old Testament provides example after example of individuals who draw destruction down upon themselves and their tribe thanks to overweening pride or ambition, and also because the Greek tradition (to name but one more) proliferates with cautionary tales of tragic figures carried away by hubris. Such figures dreamed big dreams, after the fashion that we recommend so vigorously in political speeches and commencement addresses—and then they paid the ultimate price; because, to the traditional mind, the future—not the past—is where you find graveyards.

Our typical commencement speaker at a high school graduation, honestly, would be howled off the stage if he were addressing the audience of Aeschylus. By the same token, the equanimity with which a settlement of low-tech tribesmen would have accepted a flooded village (and its multiple fatalities) would astonish us. We are outraged when a hurricane such as occurs only once a decade devastates a coastal city. Things like that aren't supposed to happen! Somebody has betrayed us—our leaders have lied to us, our engineers have hoodwinked us, our evil capitalist tycoons have changed our climate! And we rage in this fashion even though scientific study itself will have warned us that, about once every decade, our current level of preparation must prove inadequate.

I'm not terribly far beyond the half-century mark on my own earthly timeline, yet I find it shocking that the future appears to be the only direction where people look in seeking relief from their gloom. They consider the past a book not only read and closed, but read without profit and lacking any relevance to the present. To the extent that history continues to be taught in our schools, it has been rendered "useful" through polemical transformation. Now its needle points directly to the indictments and panaceas of this or that political ideology. The indissoluble mystery of human manners and motives in bygone days (once a source of fascination to me as a young student) is swatted aside as trivial clutter. *What* mystery? The struggle of the oppressed against injustice explains everything! Similarly, in popular literature and entertainment, if a knight-errant or one of Alexander's hoplites is a story's hero, he usually arrives on the scene through a "worm hole" and riding a dragon from a parallel universe; or else a meticulous producer may reconstruct Viking garb and gear or 1868 frontier firearms with minute accuracy... but the moral outlook of the characters is raspingly postmodern, all nihilism and lust for power. We can't seem to touch the past at any corner, in short, without bending it into the future.

Could it be, as well, that we consign our darkest fears about the future to some makeshift past that we pretend really existed? We dread (if only subconsciously) the influence that human nature's animal half may exert upon our terrestrial utopias and intergalactic expeditions... and so we banish all such apprehension to the world of evil Christian crusaders, of evil Southern slaveholders, of evil Nazi stormtroopers. The late Gene Roddenberry, I recently learned, made a pest of himself behind the scenes of *Star Trek: The Next Generation* because too many scripts were locating tension within the crew. This was the next generation: no one aboard any Star Fleet vessel was supposed to be capable of causing trouble! All problems, as we of the twenty-first century see it, belong either to the past or (if we're cruising the galaxy) to civilizations stuck in a past that we ourselves have left behind.

Such a slight of hand secures us a dual advantage. First, it disperses our fear without fully ignoring it, so that we may indulge ourselves in the illusion of having handled the "problem of sin".

Second, it bolsters the essential notion that the past truly was a squalid, loathsome place whose clammy touch our progressive ideals have shaken off—from whose primal Darwinian soup our more evolved consciousness has lifted us in irresistible triumph. Even so has Shelley's Prometheus shaken off his chains in this chapter's opening citation, a virtual hymn to "revolution".

Speaking of Darwin… the evolutionary perspective, with its cruel dependency upon the survival of the fittest, is an indispensable component of our "future-worship", I think. We could not so cavalierly wave aside the past if we did not thoroughly convince ourselves of its unworthiness, its bestiality. I'm tempted to conjecture that scorn for the past is rooted in our footloose, high-tech lifestyle, where old skills are forever yielding to new ones, where citizens are forever wandering in search of new jobs, and where the foundations of stable communities are thus forever being overturned. I made precisely this case a few pages back—and it's a valid case, up to a point; but I believe an even deeper commitment—a psychic commitment—to linear change may underlie such circumstantial commitments forced upon us by the technician's semi-nomadic career path.

Recall the lonely figure in a Friedrich painting who gazes into a sublime alpine chasm; and recall, as well, that I warned of his peak's opposing slope. The prospect of history's almost infinite succession of empires and glories come and gone beckons the spirit to rise above its earthly bonds, with their invincible ties to futility... but it also, in a manner so subtle that the meditative loner probably never senses himself being seduced, implies the possibility of a great staircase. All of those past eras and epochs, their wave-like restlessness carrying human civilizations through crests and troughs... and what does it amount to? Abiding misery. But why? If the past's failures stretch out farther than the eye can see, may not the future's efforts at correction stretch out equally far—or even farther? And how can material reality resist the labor of our species' tireless persistence? And how can we in the present not devote ourselves to that labor when we see that the past has prepared nothing for us but an open grave?

I think it no accident that Charles Darwin's theory emerged in the wake of such robust speculations on the part of the later Romantics— the dynamos who touched off a series of revolutions in Western Europe. (Jean-Baptiste Lamarque was pecking around the central notions of evolutionary theory years before Darwin; and even Kant had written an essay wherein he pondered the curious fact that human racial characteristics appeared to have adapted physically to different climates.) The Romantic vision of the individual soul's liberation from its social, cultural, and corporeal chains had indeed catalyzed a hunger to promote the Rights of Man—the right of every man (and woman) to live as an autonomous being endowed by God with free will, not as a slave to times, customs, and circumstances. Once this energy was released, however, I'm afraid it swept our forefathers into rather too idealistic an estimate of life's potential. Riding upon sublime exhilaration, our soul may touch the throne of God; but our body remains earth-bound, where its parameters for mapping out fifty or sixty years of activity are quite constricted. The past, in fact, indicates most of those parameters very well on everyone's map.

I must not conclude this woefully tight encapsulation of immensely complex cultural factors by cutting more corners than absolutely necessary; and to avoid needless mutilation, I will add that Darwin's theory is, of course, scarcely a direct expression of the Romantic spirit. Yet it is indirectly so, I suspect, in the same way that the bleak authors of mid-nineteenth-century Realism are wounded Romantics. The political revolutions earlier in the century had largely failed, at least for the time being. Sometimes they had sabotaged their own high mission, as when Napoleon had had himself crowned emperor (on which occasion Beethoven could hardly be restrained from shredding his Third Symphony, dedicated to the Liberator). The past, it appeared, wasn't ready to relinquish its hold upon human institutions. Social classes remained, hereditary privilege remained, poverty and oppression remained... the world was sliding back down the slope that had just been ascended rather than exploring the mountain's far side. The legacy of yesteryear, naturally, seemed more baleful than ever in this atmosphere—but the future's brilliant hopes had grown all but unreachable.

Progress: how could it be made? Delacroix's luxuriantly homicidal canvases show us in graphic detail a few years before Darwin explains the mechanism. The customs and manners in which entire societies had been so rigorously conditioned had to be stripped away, stripped to the bone. Raw, ruthless energy was required. Otherwise, the squeamishness of artificial progress—the brainwash of superficial "humanity"—would forever hold the species circling in the same eddy. Nature, brutal though she seemed, pointed the way forward. Cast off all inhibition and take a pledge to follow animal nature.

The fittest would survive—yes, and they would create a new "second nature" which would leave men dedicated to a never-before-seen kind of society rather than numbed to wear the shackles of the old one. A sublimely fearful creative force was needed, drawn from the energy of the thundercloud and the tsunami... Beethoven again, but without the harmony—purged of *ancien régime* influences to yield the explosive cacophony of Stravinsky....

Wait, now. Am I talking about Darwin, or about Marx? I believe I'm talking about both.

What you can't see—and really must see—in Eugène Delacroix's *Death of Sardanapalus* is the rich reds integrating the king's bed cover, the rug on which his harem is being slain, the rearing horse's gear, and the head scarf of the Moor trying to control the steed… and never a drop of blood anywhere. The luxuriance of the scene more resembles a festive debauch than a murderous slaughter. The doomed monarch's boredom at the lurid collapse of his world and his own imminent death seems reflected in the painter's attention to the scene's sumptuous aesthetics rather than to its moral atrocity. Is not Delacroix suggesting that the humane conventions restricting behavior (what my generation would have called "hang-ups" back in the Sixties) need to go? Is there not a touch of Charles Manson in this magnificent but spiritually bankrupt style?

CHAPTER FIVE

Worship of the Future as Dangerous Lunacy

Those who promise us paradise on earth never produced anything but a hell.
Karl Popper

The moments I volunteered earlier as examples of transcended linear time were mostly recollections. Certainly those of the personal variety were drawn from an overview of past events, where they stood out with unique clarity. I've no doubt that some people are better suited than I to recognizing these special moments even as they occur. I would conjecture that because I am suspicious of anything smacking of the mystical (probably due to a brief overdose on the "charismatic" during my twenties), I bring too much skepticism to each day's tasks for the numinous to take me easily by storm. I used to have that "outside of time" feeling in the presence of beautiful music. I would know instantly that I had heard something destined to stay in my mind for the rest of my life, unaffected by the passing years—and I could summon up several pieces of that order right now. They are always with me. Yet for that very reason, I have all but ceased to listen to music. I find so much of the contemporary world adversarial and cutthroat that I seem to have developed a subconscious fear of being left unprepared against the daily gamut of assaults. As an ancient samurai once wrote, you enter a war zone as soon as you leave your home's threshold. Listening to great music—for me—produces the risk of not reacting fast enough to the next incoming arrow or spear.

Yet people less neurotic than I quite often probably "just know" when they've entered a moment that is more than a point on a chronological line segment. And now that I'm retired, I, too, am frequently able to find such moments in the sky overhead: when I catch the clouds streaked or mottled in rose as the sun rises on my farm, for instance, or when I spy the full moon creeping up behind pine needles at dusk. I didn't have easy access to nature while I was on the job; and if I'd had such access, I would likely have given it the same cold shoulder as I turned to music. Especially since being a college professor was supposed to have been a liberation into a world of free thinking and open expression, the practical fact of its being a snake pit filled with power struggles, political assassinations, and thought-policing "PC" ambushes required me to bear down—to make sure that my samurai sword was ever loose in its scabbard. No, the contemporary campus is *not* a place conducive to appreciating the beautiful, the sublime, and the eternal!

Having acknowledged my own ineptitude at playing the mystic, I will hasten to add that there's nothing particularly personal in my dread of projecting transcendent experiences into the future. In fact, I can state the case very objectively here. Idolatry of the future is precisely what has made college humanities programs the spiritual sinkholes that they have become. Obviously, after making a claim like that, I have much explaining to do—and I shall now do it.

To invest events with a numinous (i.e., timeless, bigger-than-life) quality before they even occur is insanity. In a child, it's probably normal and endearing; but children are under the care of adults (let us hope), and the adult needs to shake off any such adoration of tomorrow. The child leaps from bed on Christmas morning hoping for magic. Little by little, year after year, he discovers that there's no Santa Claus, and that nothing within the bright wrappers will ever completely fulfill his expectations. Sad, yes... but normal. The adult, in the "spiritually best-case" scenario, learns to shift such expectation to a source beyond this material world. The cultural lesson of Christmas is not meant to be that "everything's a crock, and you're always getting screwed by appearances"—no, that's not it! The idea, rather, is that the maturing child should learn to shift his divination of something too grand for this world's boundaries into an emerging consciousness of another, higher world. Of course, as we energetically filter any hint of Christian faith from Christmas (or "the holidays"), the chances diminish that such a message gets clearly transmitted through all the worldly static.

This unhappy condition proceeds to yield generations of adults still waiting—in ever more surly aspect—for Santa Claus. I have known young men and women to embark upon blind dates or computer-assisted matches with the resolution, "I'm sick of being single: I'm going to marry this next one, no matter what!" The results are not uplifting. Many college students take a similar approach to selecting a major: that is, having wasted at least a year sampling disciplines that proved less satisfying than they'd hoped for, they vow, "At least I know that nurses [engineers, pharmacists] can find jobs and make good money. With a fat bank account, I can console myself over the weekend for the other five days." Santa doesn't travel down that chimney, either.

When you depend upon a "special tomorrow" to lift you off the daily treadmill, you run grave risk of doing one or both of two disastrous things. The first is that you may passively attempt to reshape tomorrow as it becomes today by selectively perceiving its details. You magnify its good qualities and squint at its bad ones until they disappear. Your date is no longer a shallow person with vulgar tastes, but a refined, sensitive spirit who just needs to be properly understood. Your Marketing major might seem like a cynical program of tricks designed to sell anything to anybody... but you'll be fine with it, because you will only work for virtuous companies that never bend the truth! (I could use the advice of a good marketer, by the way: I'm only suggesting that people whose nature balks at any sort of manipulation shouldn't deceive themselves about this field's being a good match with their temperament.)

Forgive me if I propose an analogy from baseball for the sake of making the issue very tangible. A professional hitter doesn't wave at the center-field bleachers, as the legendary Babe Ruth is supposed to have done (but didn't really do) in the 1932 World Series, and announce that he's about to stroke a home run. Instead, he concentrates upon making solid contact, driving through the heart of the ball with a level swing that takes his barrel into a crisp collision. He chases the afternoon's previous two strikeouts from his mind completely, and he utterly ignores the incidental detail that a homer just now would win the game. Any such preoccupation with past or future events would draw his concentration away from the present; and, indeed, even any sharing of the present's focus with the crowd's cheers or teammates' exhortations can only prove a distraction. By allowing himself to be absorbed wholly into the task of the instant, on the other hand, he stands the best chance of satisfying all of those peripheral goals: of creating an indelible memory, of turning the future gold, of winning the game, of thrilling crowd and teammates... but none of it will happen if he doesn't dedicate every particle of his being, body and spirit, to that micro-second of meeting the pitch squarely.

Or permit me (though here the hazard of alienating readers is even greater) to draw a very specific example from current political issues. Say that we have a refugee population massing upon our borders with hundreds of children in their midst. No decent human being stands by idly as children suffer. Therefore... therefore, we forge ahead to create a future of universal safety and health for all refugee children! We dissolve all laws and ignore all protocols governing the admission of aliens into our nation. We impatiently, even indignantly sweep aside all timid, caviling half-hearters who want us to admit some but not all, to admit at a slower pace, etc., etc. The ideal of perfect bliss beckons us just up the road. We have to get there from here: any little obstacles along the way need simply to be kicked aside.

As a result, we have new diseases spreading among our own children. We have overstrained public resources being doled out with increasing inadequacy to a growing mass of recipients. We have diminishing employment opportunities for the new arrivals in urban settings where overpopulated inner-city areas see crime and gang activity rise. Traffic escalates. Pollution mounts. Roads and other infrastructural provisions deteriorate. Public resentment stirs. The new refugee communities become balkanized islands within the broader society where children learn mainstream language and culture at ever more deficient rates. A sub-class develops whose prospects look distinctly bleaker than they would have been back in the old country, where the cultural environment was monolithic, the network of extended family sizable, and the means of keeping body and soul together tried-and-true (however meager). And then... well, let the criminal element that passes unnoticed amid the spate of *simpatico* refugees be a topic for another day. Its presence might be negligible in some cases—though, in this fallen world, I've found no instance where that claim is justified.

Through suppressing tremendously consequential details as if they were mere attempts to tarnish our glittering vision, we create for the very people we longed to assist a veritable hell on earth. The present moment had that within its contours and colors which didn't look like the marble temple we had imagined... and so we worked over and around the unresponsive material. Then we stood back and, quite probably (if my experience of fair-weather good Samaritans is accurate), dusted off our hands, congratulated ourselves on a job well done, turned our backs on abiding problems that threatened to topple the edifice, and blamed the uncooperative among us for mismanagement when we heard a terrific collapse from the safety of our exclusive neighborhoods.

This is one utterly ruinous consequence of projecting "higher moments" into the future: we put the perfect home-run swing on a pitch that falls a foot beneath the reach of our bat.

The other peril of "future-worship" appears when we actively intervene in the clearly impending catastrophe of our folly. We strive to make others "cooperate" whose contrary opinions hold us back. The friend who tries to warn us away from marrying the person we decided upon after one date is no longer a friend—not unless he changes his tune. The parent who observes, "How can you become a nurse when the sight of blood makes you faint?" receives no further visits unless he or she admits to having made a foolish, unproductive comment.

The population into which a refugee mass is not being successfully integrated is taxed more heavily to supply the newcomers' needs and reproached for being "racist" or "xenophobic" if it raises a protest. Its members are ordered to adapt their cultural ways, to mingle better—to learn a new language, to embrace a new religion. Recalcitrants who publish dissenting editorials are charged with "hate speech". Repeat-offenders are fined and sent off to "re-education camp". Public agencies that generate alarming crime statistics are menaced with budget-slashing—in response to which menace, peace officers are commanded by their superiors to make fewer arrests and to log infractions in less "offensive" categories. A once free republic veers in the direction of Orwell's *Nineteen Eighty-Four*, where two and two equal five. The formerly well-meaning moral luminaries of society look more and more like oppressive despots.

Seeking after the "divine moment" in the future distorts our best impulses to horrible caricature. What might have been the inspiration for a good deed in the present becomes the genesis of wicked habits capable of stunting an entire society's growth. We come to dwell in a fantasy whose golden glow warms our soul, but whose perversion of our behavior in the real world leaves us dead to the reality created for us by God. Our only defense against the charge of being outright evil-doers might be that we have stumbled into lunacy; and, indeed, perhaps Socrates was right that there is no significant difference between the two.

CHAPTER SIX

How Worship of the Future Has Destroyed the Arts

You ask the pattern of failure and success?
A fisherman's song reaches deep over the shore.
Wang Wei

My first examples of moments "dislocated from linear time" owed much to artistic representation. Immanuel Kant wouldn't have agreed that the genuinely sublime could be portrayed by paint on canvas, and he never heard Beethoven performed; but his disciple Friedrich Schiller certainly believed that drama could be sublime when staging the self-surpassing feats of a brave, soulful person pushed beyond all ordinary limits. These days, we don't much care about distinguishing between sublimity and beauty. It's not as though we exist any longer in an envelope of tidily contained, mathematically calibrated chamber music and canvases of still-life settings.

In fact, *these days* I should be hard pressed to say just what we ever produce of beauty. I used to hear, almost incidentally, some of the scores that the late British composer Geoffrey Burgon wrote for BBC serials—and my admiration would be instant, perhaps one of those "moments". (Burgon's theme for the serialization of John le Carré's *Tinker, Tailor, Soldier, Spy* will never leave me.) Perhaps Sir Roger Scruton has such talents in mind when he insists that his countrymen are reviving art by discovering the religious dimension of music.

As a teacher of literature for thirty-five years, however, and a lifelong enthusiast for the well-written word, I have to say that the bleak landscape I perceive in the arts is pretty disheartening. If only it were merely bleak! If only one didn't see urine-filled jars containing a Crucifix being passed off as art and heralded in big-city exhibits! If only putative outlines of the Madonna worked in cow dung weren't hanging along the same corridors a month later! Or if only a rather whiney diary relating a Sioux girl's discomfort with the Quaker education lavished upon her were not memorialized in college literary anthologies as a classic of the Native American/feminist struggle! Zitkála-Sá was no Aleksandr Solzhenitsyn, either in her degree of suffering or in her literary talent; but undergraduates today are much more likely to know the former name than the latter. Nevertheless, the students of one survey class that I observed were laughing under their breath at the "find the exploitation" game through which their instructor was leading them as she taught Zitkála-Sá's chronicle of victimization. It's a safe bet that few of them left college with a hunger to read more "literature".

Well, perhaps you can understand why I retreated to personal experience in seeking examples of a lived moment distinct from other moments before and after it, as if lifted from linear time. For, in a way, I was seeking beauty: not just that, or not even primarily that—but, after all, the sense of "God is here" has much in common with the sense of "here isn't just here". Religious adoration and love of artistic beauty have—or should have, and used to have—much in common. Sir Roger, obviously, has noticed as much. We all notice it, surely, if we stop to think about the importance of architecture and music to our religious services. Every personal experience that I described in Chapter Three might readily be refashioned into something poetic, if not something suitable for painting. My memory of my mother's listening to a cardinal would probably be least susceptible to the paintbrush (though the bright red songster would make quite a splash in the dense crape myrtle). What I wanted to emphasize about that occasion, remember, wasn't anything picturesque in the scene: The undying image in my mind was orbiting the brief, fragile happiness of a person to whom happiness didn't come easily. The occasion, then, possessed complexity for me. Even enigma. My mother must, of course, have wished to be happy; who doesn't? That instant proved her capable of happiness, at least in some variety. What became lost, then, in the transition from a chirpy thrush in a shrub to the human world of tight, intense connections and obligations? Did adult life, or family life, or civilized life, exert such a throttle-hold upon this young matron? And if it was so for her, *why* was it so—and for how many others was it so?

Here the contemporary literary scholar would come bursting through the door of my questions like a SWAT team, explosive answer locked and loaded. *All Western women are oppressed! The white male patriarchy has wrought this ruin! Destroy! Crush! Wipe the slate clean! Revolution!*

No... no, I don't think your revolution will return us to the cardinal's song as a point of departure—and will certainly not carry us there as a destination. The only thing that exploding the scene in this manner accomplishes (I've used a form of the word "explode" twice now: you can't avoid it when describing today's "scholarship") is to signify that my mother wasn't where she wanted to be. Exploding her circumstances, however, wouldn't necessarily land her—what remained of her—in better ones. In fact, I'm sure it wouldn't. Her response to complete transformation would have been, "Not back there... but not here, either." Indeed, that would be the response of virtually every feminist who has ever penned a diatribe against Western civilization. They hate where they are... so would they rather be wearing a hijab and sharing a residence with two younger wives? Or would they rather be CEO's, every one, with vast amounts of that Western affluence they claim to deplore—but no child to visit them on their lonely holidays as they near retirement?

N'importe où, hors du monde, opined the French poet Baudelaire wryly of his own day's bored bourgeoisie: "Take me anywhere at all... just so it's not in this world."

Because, you see, that's exactly what great art keeps telling us, and also what the numinous moment slaps across our face: we are not of this world. We are in it, condemned to it for a while, confined to thinking in its terms—but not to *feeling* in those terms, because our souls remain elsewhere. So we produce art. We arrange the things of this world in ways that point us out of this world. We cannot express why our happiness is stained with sadness, why our grief conceals relief and even hope: such conundrums can't be resolved with worldly logic. We always want something more, something other, when we touch something of this world that we had imagined ourselves desperately to want. The "job of a lifetime" disappoints, and the king's ransom that it pays cannot buy enough toys and conveniences to supply the missing part. The soulmate whom we had supposed ourselves to be marrying doesn't really understand us, and even our children grow into ingrates and go their own way. Nothing is ever the *something*. The void always persists.

And the "moment" tells us, in a flash of strange code, that the absent piece is here, was always here—but that we can't fully see it because it is not fully here. The moment wrenches us aside from our linear trek deeper and deeper into a futile earthly quest, insisting that we stop, lean back, and turn our gaze from side to side: the same action as is elicited by one of those sublime seascapes.

To any such defense of art, the academy smiles and quips that we're merely kicking the can down the road—as indeed we are, and as indeed academics do themselves; but their "postponement" is not of an order that draws them outside of linear time. Hence they are free to scoff at the "Western bourgeois" penchant (not really Western or bourgeois, but human) for investing objects and rituals with more value than their material reality can bear. The benighted classes (sigh the scholars with a sneer) cannot see that the power structure has bred them to honor certain icons and pour reverence into certain routines that have firmly ensconced the authoritarian class in its lofty seat. Liberation involves freeing oneself from all such adoration of objects as vehicles of mysterious value. A thing is just a thing. Everything is just nothing. And in the complete and ultimate meaninglessness of life, the liberated mind is free to place its own value wherever it wants.

Explosion again. In that snowstorm of red feathers that can no longer sing, we have liberation into utter relativism. *Fays ce que voudras*, reads the device above Rabelais's burlesque monastery: "Do whatever you like." Or, in the words of the Ivory Tower's Father Superior, Jacques Derrida, "Always already." Every circle you try to open upon reality is already doomed to close as soon as your pencil touches paper. You're trapped—we're trapped: so why not at least treat every border with the contempt it deserves? (Strange, how this guru's name dovetails into the English word "deride": I'm sure the old nihilist would have found that trick of fate quite a tantalizing subject for his incessantly circling pen.)

Derrida and some of his deconstructive mates, at least, seemed to appreciate (somewhat... sometimes) that freedom from all stricture is the most suffocating servitude. The human mind cannot breathe in such a leaden coffin. It must create space by defining not-space... but where is any space left for a doodling pencil to play with?

In the future, of course. Kick the can *far* down the road this time. Now that the contemporary intellectual (or intellectualist) has exploded all the complexity out of any possible experience, present or past, the one remaining locus where transformation might take place—where our "mean nothing" lives might begin to mean *something*—is the future. And we can give that future any shape we like. Since all of the so-called "values" that hampered us in the past are mere cultural programming designed to keep us in chains, we can rewrite the program—from the bottom up—once we throw off the chains. Future man, or woman, or mwaman, will bear no fetuses at all—or will rip a perfect baby from his/her/zer thigh like Zeus birthing Dionysus. This brave new being will visit far planets and thrive on toxic gases, tying purple clouds into bows or burrowing a mile through the permafrost on a whim. The only literature that can chase after such supernatural steps is science fiction; yet the best science fiction of the past, confined as it was by a human nature ever assertive beneath layers of miraculous technology, must itself be rewritten. Raw will is free to wander without encountering any inhibitive consequences to its choices. The full-blown Hell of this lunatic conception is supposed to be Paradise.

And herein lies the terminal paradox that the Derrida brigade seems unable to absorb in its ecstasy. Since human nature is not, in fact, a figment of the patriarchal imagination, the design of the *Übermensch* must forever keep running into the murderously tight parameters of its will to power. Every time, in other words, that the New Being cannot do one thing because it's doing another thing, the unfortunate representatives of the other thing—which was yesterday's new thing—become the targets of the new-new firing squad. I think again of Gene Roddenberry's insane vexation with his next generation of *Star Trek* writers who couldn't seem to distill every last trace of Original Sin from their characters. No more sin! No! All future conflict will be transferred to upright green reptiles who still worship a stone deity, or to some other lagging troglodyte tribe in need of liberation. The enemy is *not* us—it is everyone around us who impedes us from becoming more of our destined Higher Self.

Such lunacy, I need hardly add, explains much about our poisonous political climate. Those who cling to anything of the past (as represented by the Constitution, religion, or even public promises) are the dark forces that threaten to plunge us back into nothingness. We must be free from all past restrictions so that we may boldly go where no being has gone before... and we must *all* go there in lock-step, because resistance slows down progress. It allows the stench of death to catch up with our gallop. No delay is good delay! The notion of promise is itself an absurdity—for how can you pledge yourself to any course of action today, when tomorrow your being will have evolved further and your higher form's keener inspiration will have suggested a better course of action? I think now not so much of Roddenberry, but more of Stalin forever exiling or executing his own soldiers because they had seen too much of the outside world.

Our literature, history, and philosophy departments are selling this loco-weed around the nation in colleges and universities. My imitation of a feminist response to my mother's pleasure in a singing cardinal was no parody. This is what goes on where literature is "studied". Virgil's *Aeneid* is "sexist" because Juno is always in a jealous rage. Dante's three great poems are so because his females (even among the damned, like Francesca) seem gentle and yielding rather than robust and full of initiative. Milton's *Paradise Lost* is so because the figure of Eve is insipid and flirtatious. It's not that such critical observations wholly lack grounding. The problem is that analysis stops with a single superficial observation, first rating the entire work along the "woke to women's rights" spectrum—and then discarding it when the "feminometer" reading is too low. Not a thought given to shadows and echoes—to the sense of something other than what's immediately before the eye; for to chase any echo beyond the surface is to be sucked in by patriarchal propaganda. We must on no account allow ourselves to be "charmed"!

A university education of this nature—a rigid programming of all one's thoughts, so that one is fitted with inflexible blinders and can henceforth travel only along the linear progressive tunnel—is a death sentence to spiritual life. Young people who feel drawn to powerful art should seriously consider majoring in Mathematics or Accounting rather than in English; but beyond that, any person who would like to discover a higher meaning to life (i.e., any sane adult) should avoid the demoralizing infection of inhuman futuristic fantasies. A healthy future can be negotiated only when one takes stable bearings upon references that don't constantly shift. To attempt building a future, instead, upon as-yet-only-imagined "realities" is a straight road to perpetual misery for oneself and every unlucky person within one's sphere.

CHAPTER SEVEN

Stable Identity vs. Getting Lost in the Tunnel

Compare yourself to who you were yesterday, not to who someone else is today.
Jordan Peterson's Fourth Rule for Life

I'm among Dr. Peterson's millions of admirers. Several people urged me almost at the same time to view his YouTube videos—which, of course, I eventually did. If ever there were an academic who would refuse to deliver the standard commencement speech at graduation— "Dream dreamily, follow your dreams, you can do anything, the world is your oyster, the future is now and it's all gilded gold"... no, Jordan Peterson is not that man. And one may say "man" in his presence without immediately falling to one's knees, pouring ash over one's head, and begging forgiveness for a slip of the tongue. There's little risk of his changing the surname to "Peterperson".

Yet someone is bound to notice that Dr. Peterson is a great believer in and promoter of self-change in the pursuit of a better future. Here I am, protesting that we too often focus dizzily upon objectives that haven't even cleared the horizon while ignoring the chasm yawning below our next step. Is the implication of my argument not that we should abstain from cultivating an idealized image of ourselves far down the road and concentrate on the landscape at our side?

Yes and no. There is a right way and a wrong way to pursue self-improvement. I intend to address matters of practical conduct much more directly in Part Two of this book. For now, imagine a person who has decided that he wishes to be less of a complainer and enjoy a more dignified reputation among his peers. Contrast him with another person who wishes to be adored by all the girls and envied by his male peers for having arrived at the peak of material success. (This is not so very distant from the wish expressed by the Greek sage Solon in a fragmentary poem of epic hexameters; tribal cultures rate being esteemed by neighbors and feared by outsiders as occupying the summit of satisfaction.)

The former of our two subjects is the more mature, as we modern Westerners see things (and I believe our culture, at its height, was more advanced in moral matters than the tribal alternative). Person Number One's aim still depends somewhat upon how others perceive him, which removes his behavior somewhat from the perfectly virtuous realm; but at least he is concerned about his dignity in a way that overlaps a desire to exert more self-control. He can take action instantly upon his resolve to complain less, whether or not others around him observe the change. The latter subject, however, longs after ends that have no plain connection to means. He could be the toast of the town by creating and patenting a new software program that diagnoses ailing babies... or he could get to the same point by running a Ponzi scheme and evading indictment. Professor Kant would say that the ends of his behavior are in fact instrumental rather than terminal: i.e., that what he wants is just a means to what he *really* wants, which is sensual pleasure and worldly power. He's another Caligula in the making.

Subject One holds the means of his improvement substantially within his own power because his concentration is upon present realities. Subject Two has very little under his own control that pertains to his imagined objective. If he's truly prepared to achieve it at any cost, then he must be considered a rather dangerous character, both to himself and to others, because his strategy could take him wherever tomorrow happens to lead.

Arranging the terrain that separates today from tomorrow by starting from tomorrow's doorstep and working backward has harmed many a human being. Sometimes it produces corpses. Too often, incompetent police detectives will decide that a certain suspect looks good for the crime and filter their evidence according to how well it squeezes the presumed perpetrator into an emerging narrative. The correct procedure is to collect and review all evidence while holding all suspects equally at arm's length—and keeping the suspect file wide-open, as well. Likewise, intelligence officers charged with national security have been known to sift through evidence of threat and discard items that point in "politically improper" directions. If they or their superiors are extremely reluctant to nourish an anti-Muslim scare, for instance, they may ignore hints of a possible terrorist act because it points to an imam. Nobody questions that the professionals in all such cases have good intentions; but when you begin writing your final report before you've even assembled the available data, people may end up dead who might have lived.

I often use the image of the tunnel to represent an excessively linear fixation upon the future. Tunnel-vision will not allow "distraction" to percolate through from the sides. The neck doesn't turn. Shades are pulled down over lateral windows. Only what's ahead counts. When the "Sixties radicals" (as they liked to style themselves) transformed the American campus, their battle cry was "relevance". They would have no more study of Homeric epic, medieval romance, Elizabethan drama, or Restoration comedy. Whatever literature and history was presented to them in class must foreground the struggles of racial minorities and women or elevate to primary importance the popular culture that amused them on TV, at the movies, and in rock bands. They demanded "studies" courses: "Studies in Chicano Poetry", "Studies in Hollywood's Black Stereotypes". They didn't want the "garbage of the past" disrupting their exclusive attention to what they found of current interest.

For some reason, our intelligentsia (largely drawn from this generation of "I want it all, I want it now" radicals) has decided to deem the Sixties a time of spiritual rebirth. The Beatles were visiting a guru in India, the Hippies were lighting up to an "alternative lifestyle"... so, obviously, we were growing more spiritual. Some of us. To my mind, the very thing so detested by the "rebels" in their middle-class parents—the commercialist focus on identifying and marketing whatever would make a buck—was painfully visible in their own behavior. No, they didn't need to worry about making a buck (thanks to their parents' expertise in such matters); yet they still had the thought-habits of someone who sifts through piles of perceptions and experiences to pull out only what strikes his fancy. They hunted for the "useful", these Flower Children... and everything else might never have existed. The "experience of love" must not be hemmed in by the convention of marriage—but the experience of chaste celibacy to keep the spirit pure of baser hungers was swept away. The "experience of freedom" must not be straitjacketed within a daily routine of chores— but the experience of dedication to a self-sacrificial mission demanding that one rise before the sun never intruded upon their lives.

In terms of the Gospels, it is when you lose yourself that you find yourself; it is when you die that you live. Throwing out present obstacles with the trash to live in an ideal state of bliss that hasn't yet been secured and can't be sustained impoverishes life. It indeed squeezes the spirituality out of all we do. Moments of higher reality overtake us as we toil away at necessary tasks, not as we pretend that we already and instantly inhabit that higher reality. If you want to tap into the feeling that the material world cannot wholly confine you, then why would you selectively immerse yourself in those special things of the material world that flatter or amuse you? If your true identity is not "John Jones, rebel against the suburbs, sometime-employee at Kinko's, Susie's current lover", but rather something that has no name in this world, then why do you plaster yourself with stickers and labels until you can't see the bell-bottoms of your trousers?

Who are you, what are you? You're what you're doing *right now*. And if you're doing nothing, then... then nothing is what you are. And if you're carrying a protest sign to secure for women the right to handle any product of their body as they like, then... then you're a mobile resting-place for placards. You're the locus of a short slogan—a stick figure with the words "freedom fighter" written brightly across its nondescript face. What you actually *did* was to make Susie pregnant without ever giving a thought to anything but your selfish pleasure; and in doing so, you did not encourage Susie to incur a possible new responsibility with her eyes open, and you also subjugated your mind and soul to carnal impulse. You did nothing that a monkey in a tree doesn't do.

When I ask what you are doing, I'm not asking what you play at doing, like your favorite actor in your favorite film. (For that matter, how many actors these days find any identity in real life between their gigs of giving voice and body to fantasy?) What is your *work*? What do you *work* at doing? For what do you exchange your lower self— your lazy bundle of unused muscle and your growling belly? To what servitude do you subjugate these slaves under your rule who are rebelling against their proper master? Where are your calluses? What stars can you still see when you roll out of bed? What's the temperature outside right now? In questions like these hides the secret of who you are.

And those are all questions about the reality that passes unnoticed across your "window upon irrelevancy"—the one you shuttered lest you ever distract your forward-straining attention. They designate material points of contact that your spirit's trajectory makes with the world—not ready-made imitations of worldly striving that you have thrust upon a stage for all to admire. You've already concocted, patented, bottled, stamped, and marketed your "meaning"... which means to me that you mean nothing; for meaning is not something that you fabricate for display, but something that takes you by surprise as you wrestle with raw materials right in front of you.

I think Dr. Peterson would agree with me. Neither of us wants you to "stay as you are" in some stiflingly sedentary sense. But what you will be isn't really distinct from what you are, either—not unless you're trying to live a fantasy. (And that doesn't constitute an exception, of course: it only means that you're losing your mind.) The question is this: do you know *being* well enough to *be* within it? Are you racing down a tunnel that narrows and narrows... or are you susceptible to getting knocked off the track from time to time?

CHAPTER EIGHT

Walking the Tightrope Across Human Paradox

*Et une à une, de contradiction dominée en contradiction dominée, je
m'achemine vers le silence des questions et ainsi la béatitude.*

And one by one, from surmounted contradiction to surmounted
contradiction, I make my way toward the silencing of questions and
thus to beatitude.　　　　　　　　　　　Antoine de Saint-Exupéry

If you didn't harbor the thought before reading the last chapter,
you're surely giving it some consideration now: why am I associating
the projection of ideas into the future with unspiritual living,
wrongdoing—even evil—while I appear to celebrate absorption in the
present moment with virtue? This stands conventional thinking about
morality on its head. People who live for the day are those who can't
be trusted, because they simply feed their appetites from hour to hour.
People who look to the future are those who abstain from riotous or
"me first" behavior, because they foresee that inconsiderate acts will
alienate them from the community. To view things otherwise isn't just
to be unconventional; it's to be irrational. Am I crazy?

First of all, my recommendation is not and has never been that we
live for the day. Indeed, I opened this book's discussion by suggesting
that we can often identify moments that "stand outside of time" only in
retrospect; so, if anything, my emphasis has been on preserving our
past experiences in higher regard. To some extent, surely, we can
import into our present actions this conservationist alertness that
"something more important may be happening than meets the eye"; and
to whatever extent we make such an adjustment to viewing the present,
I believe we have a greater chance of resisting the tunnel-vision of
"future-worship". Especially as adults whose susceptibility to the
world's supernatural wavelengths has grown dull, we might do well to
pay more attention to the reality under our fingertips than to a fantasy
incapable of reaching any flesh-and-blood receptor.

Furthermore, I would point out that behavior deserving of the
word "sinful" has a more intimate relationship with deliberate planning
than with knee-jerk reaction. You can find Dante clearly recognizing

as much (and he took his theological cue from Thomas Aquinas) in how he lays out his Inferno: sins requiring more thought are punished deeper in Hell's pit. In a more popularized version of the same notion, the Middle Ages divided the Seven Deadly Sins as follows. The sins of the flesh were gluttony, lechery, and indolence; the sins of the spirit were avarice, envy, and wrath; the so-called worldly sin was vanity (or vain pride). Now, I wouldn't necessarily favor just these terms today in writing of sin—but I certainly embrace the central point. That is, the bad behavior which flows from impulsive responses belongs to a childish mentality, while that which trickles subtly from careful calculation is full-grown corruption of the spirit.

Look at it this way. Anger is an impulse. It's a sin of which I can write with some authority, since I have battled it often. It tends to flare up before moral reason has time to be alerted and engaged. Lust is of the same order, particularly in young people. The flame is lit instantly, most often by something seen. I would class fear as another such regrettable yet instantaneous, all-but-irresistible behavior. Our fears frequently have a basis in our genetic programming, or so sociologists like Dr. Peterson tell us; and at that level, they probably have our preservation as an objective. Only through reflection can we short-circuit the message and tell Mother Nature, "There are things more important to me than my physical survival. Please back off!"

You may recall that, in discussing eighteenth-century philosophy's conception of the sublime in art, I noted the necessity of fear's being absent from the perceiver's mind. The prospect of a restless ocean isn't sublime to a castaway who worries that each new wave may sink his raft. The reason for this exclusion is that the mind must be free of impulsive, visceral anxiety if it is to enjoy a leisurely meditation on the body's puniness and the soul's immensity. The castaway doesn't have such leisure: he's hanging on for dear life. In the artistic realm, therefore, it's clear that impulsive emotion is the outright enemy of receiving the divine moment's full impact. This is true across the board, whenever such emotion intrudes upon our efforts to register a numinous moment's fullness. When DNA hardwiring takes over, our mind shuts down and our spirit's portal of operation upon the world closes up tight.

Other sins, such as envying what our neighbors have and wishing we could turn the tables to excite envy in them, need a while to bury their roots into our heart's darker places. The worst of all sins belonging to this category, for my money, are egotism (equivalent to vanity) and megalomania (lust for power: *libido dominandi*). Medieval commentators styled the overactive ego, or vain pride, as the unique worldly sin, I suppose, because it torments all of us in our relationships with others. One cannot participate in human society without sometimes hearing a small, malign voice whispering that one isn't getting enough respect. (Actually, the path of the anchorite, or monastic hermit, was intended to be an escape route from vanity, and it might have been so... a thousand years ago. Nowadays, unoccupied desert islands are a very rare commodity.)

Thinking, in short, can produce deeper darkness as well as brighter light. When people add deliberation to the vicious impulses three paragraphs back, they sometimes make a bad situation much worse. Anger in which reflection intervenes may produce a heightened sense of perspective and a genuine change in frame of mind... but the collaboration may also form a wickedly vengeful design. Lust arrested by reflection may draw a disciplined person into a good-humored retreat, where he concedes to a woman her special and very visible qualities but decides not to react like a fish to bait. On the other hand, an undisciplined mind may form an alliance with impulse and start plotting how to get the fair one behind a locked door somewhere.

It's a pretty easily verified fact that historical figures eaten up by vanity and megalomania tend, as well, to develop a taste for the lower vices of impulse. The supreme autocrat seduces the wives of his cabinet ministers and angrily executes courtiers who don't salute him in just the right way. Dionysius of Syracuse was a classic study in paranoia. So afraid of assassination was he that his sleeping arrangements became incredibly elaborate—and he is the author of the Sword of Damocles incident in response to a bland flatterer's gushing over what a blessed life so mighty a ruler must lead. The reverse cannot be said: people disposed to fly off the handle or to grope voluptuous beauties rarely morph into tyrants. In fact, if they are truly given to such impulsive outbursts, they may well find their way up the staircase of power sealed off by that very impulsiveness.

So, no, I'm not inclined to yield the point that those who are forward-looking will likely have a higher claim to virtue. Depending on how we define "forward-looking", I would probably argue the opposite. May I stress yet again, though, that foresight is not the fly in the ointment? Anticipating others' responses is characteristic of a mature, sensitive mind. What I would warn us all against is our cultural penchant for imagining a particular future and then living out today as if our fictional tomorrow were already a reality. It should be obvious that such behavior is apt to be anything but sensitive and courteous to others. On the contrary, it effaces others from existence. We bandy the word "narcissism" about too carelessly these days, but I'm sure that we generally have this type of "bulldozing" indifference to others' feelings and concerns in mind when we use it.

I love the Saint-Exupery citation above (from the aviator-poet's unfinished work *Citadelle*) because I have long believed that every profound truth about human beings is a paradox. We make sense, all right... but only after one wades through several superficial layers in us that don't make any sense at all. We want to be foresightful, but we instead end up being fantastical. We disdain those who serve their momentary pleasure, but we substitute a program of living that merely ensures a steady supply of such pleasures discreetly concealed. We can't distinguish between living *in the moment* and living *for the day*. Our language constantly weaves snares for us, into which we step up to the knee and from which we refuse to extricate ourselves, even though liberation would be as easy as admitting, "That's not what I meant."

I'll close this chapter's brief *apologia* by deflecting one more truism that I can well imagine a critic tossing my way. I have known people to deride my "paleo" notions almost in these very terms: "Only an idiot or a tree-hugger would argue that yesterday was better than today! Our progressive lifestyle has put years on the lives of those who suffer from heart disease and cancer. Diabetics now have a normal existence. Amputees go through the day with prosthetic limbs even better, in some ways, than the original ones. In cold climates, we have heating; in hot ones, we have air conditioning. Modern agricultural methods keep millions from starving every year. Why would anyone be so brainless or so heartless as to throw into doubt the progress we have made?"

Classification as an idiot is relative, I suppose: I'm disinclined to accept it of myself in the company of most people I know. As for hugging trees, the bark I love most is that of the saplings I plant, not of the old warriors whose time to fall has come—for my nurslings will feed me, God willing, when the world of "progress" doesn't quite fulfill lofty expectations. Heart disease? Cancer? These scourges were rare when our ancestors manually labored in their fields; and suicide, by the way—whose shadow upon our population grows longer and longer—was once practically unheard-of except as a means of escaping an invader's tortures.

Granted, there's no disputing that life expectancy has grown stride for stride with our technology. After indulging a lugubrious habit of poking among ancient cemeteries in Ireland, however, I came to realize that populations of yesteryear tended to fare well if they could just get past certain choke-points. The early childbearing years were a major obstacle for women. Delivery took place in appallingly unsanitary conditions, with the midwife rarely even washing her hands. For men, the "kill zone" appeared to stretch from the mid-twenties to the late thirties. These were the years when males at their acme of strength would have tackled the most dangerous jobs around large farm animals, beneath the cliffs of quarries, in unsteady curraghs tossing upon the sea, and so forth. If older men did the same work for a while, they did it with greater knowledge of how to stay safe. Infant mortality, naturally, was also very high—yet I need hardly say that we don't reckon unwanted babies who never make it out of the womb among our contemporary fatalities. If we did, I'm not sure the survival ratio would remain in our favor.

In other words, if allowance is made for abysmal ignorance of a few basic medical protocols and for a kind of manual labor that was most risky in the early stages of industrialization, the statistical inferiority of yesteryear to today largely disappears. It isn't at all clear to me that we're happier and healthier: I am guilty as charged. And if we proceed to factor in certain frightful hazards of our technology that most of us prefer to ignore, then the advantage may just shift to our great-grandparents. I won't mention Chernobyl or Fukushima, though both are excellent examples (by the way) of "forward thinking" disastrously compromised by human arrogance. At the moment, of much greater concern to me is our utter dependency on a power grid that supplies us with food and water delivery, food and water treatment, communication, transportation, emergency services, security, lighting, entertainment, the forever-celebrated heating and air conditioning... everything we need to live, and most of what we appear to live for. This could all vanish in the wake of a massive solar flare or as a result of a shift in the earth's magnetosphere. Suddenly, one side of the balance sheet will be filled by a column of blanks; and eventually, if you survive for half a year, you'll be wishing that you knew as much about medicine as that dirty-handed midwife.

For the umpteenth time, however, I am not recommending that we all turn "survivalist". I have dedicated this work to considering the state of our spirituality. The relevance of the foregoing few paragraphs to that subject is just this. By staking our lives and our children's lives, pridefully and stupidly, on a high-tech manner of existence that we understand less and less, we are increasingly worshiping at the altar of the future. We must continue to explore the artifice of technology, without question. Should wicked regimes around the world surpass us in these skills, they may prove at least as deadly as a solar flare. Yet as we proceed, we must we keep our eyes wide open. Not only must we not blind ourselves to catastrophic risks attendant upon wondrous innovations; we must indeed train ourselves to scour the terrain to the side of each step forward. Focusing only on the horizon will land us in a ditch, as was said to have happened to Thales one night while he strutted about examining the stars.

The warning I've just issued is existential... and, of course, there's no moral obligation to survive in this world. There may sometimes be an obligation to scorn survival and sacrifice our brief life in the flesh for higher things. But arrogant complacency and dazed comfort in an abstracted fantasy don't constitute a "higher thing", do they? If we perish materially through allowing ourselves to be persuaded that we're all cadets on the Starship *Enterprise*, then the ultimate cause of our demise will prove spiritual in this way only: it will be owed to our *absence of spirituality*. We need to appreciate the creation in which we were placed by God before we start playing in a paradise of our own imagination... and, yes, I should really write "instead of" rather than "before".

CHAPTER NINE

Science's Perpetually Inconclusive Verdict on Time

> To climb out of the pit, the man knows he needs a ladder. Unmoved by the
> severity of his difficulty, the man goes home and gets a ladder out of his
> garage, walks back to the pit, climbs back in, sets up the ladder, and climbs
> out of the hole. The ladder from his garage was just the ticket, but my story
> begs an obvious question: how did the man get out of the pit in the first
> place in order to fetch the ladder? Stephen C. Meyer

I should perhaps have begun this book with the present chapter. My wish was to foreground the issue of spirituality, and to draw early attention to how effectively our spiritual life is eroded when we embrace a progressivist vision—a cultic faith in its own right, really—of the "ever better tomorrow". I pursued my chosen course, however, despite substantial risk of being poorly understood. I realized that, to the typical onlooker, playing fast and loose with cause-and-effect would appear a bit unhinged. After all, if we take one scientifically valid step, and then we follow it with another, and another... well, why *shouldn't* we end up in a better place? And even if we abstain from climbing the high-tech staircase (i.e., that of applied science), how could we ever resist thinking of time as a linear chain? How can we imagine it to be other than what it is—for is time not a straight succession of events?

We cannot resist the linear view of time, to be sure; but the reason is more because our minds are designed to arrange events in this manner than because objective links really hold them in the causal connections we suppose to lie within them. The Scots philosopher David Hume created quite a stir in the mid-eighteenth century when he proposed that causal connection is perceived through induction—through habit, that is—rather than through the discovery of any force having an independent reality. Hume overplayed his hand, no doubt. Yet it isn't hard to find daily examples of our subconsciously imposing on events certain linear connections that, as we later understand, don't exist. Say that you hear a big boom down the street and look up to find smoke rolling from above your neighbor's backyard fence. Your immediate response is to fear a terrible domestic accident of some kind.

After investigation, though, you realize that the neighbor had been grilling steaks for some while—unknown to you—and that what turned your attention in his direction was a car backfiring in the street just beyond his house.

I wrote a few pages back about the errors that unprofessional detectives make when they try to "create a narrative" by picking and choosing through the evidence instead of following every lead meticulously. (I published a book-length discussion last year of one such case—Buddy Woodall's—that sent an innocent man to prison for life.) Sometimes investigators will perceive stray bits of information scattered along a timeline and show themselves unable to resist tying the loose ends together. X needed money; Y was murdered for money. Y was shot with a .22 Glock. X's father possessed a .22 Glock that was stolen from him just weeks before the murder. Causes and effects start swarming all over the place like goldfish in a bowl where you've sprinkled a few crumbs. The results "make sense"—too much sense. They squeeze the nuance and indeterminacy right out of life and leave us with a flat script written for a B crime drama.

Post hoc, ergo propter hoc is the Latin moniker of perhaps our most common logical fallacy when handling time: "afterward, therefore because of". A good example of such erroneous reasoning might be the tribal society that exiles a newcomer to the village because bad things have been happening ever since the stranger's arrival. Lame Elk was taken in because he was a quiet, gentle young orphan who worked well with horses; but in the six months since he joined the tribe, Yellow Cloud's teepee burned down, Long Runner's mother died suddenly, and the buffalo have failed to make their annual appearance at Ragged Gap. Lame Elk is a jinx. He is cursed by the gods... he *must* be. Look at his own unhappy life. Simple cause and effect.

I recall proposing earlier that science bears some responsibility for luring our culture into the tunnel-vision of progressive thinking—but that formula needs adjustment. Genuine science actually battles against our human predisposition to arrange events in a neat causal chain. My hypothetical in the previous paragraph is meant to characterize cultures at a pre-scientific stage. It could just as well portray children whose minds are undisciplined by principles of objectivity (for children, too, are prone to single out certain suspects as "jinxes" in a riot of superstitious thinking). The true scientist continually restrains the public from supposing a cause-and-effect relationship too hastily. We are regularly told, for instance, that "ninety-eight percent of scientists" endorse the theory of global warming, or of climate change... or of some weather-related shift in our environmental circumstances yet to be adequately named. Yet certain members of the public seem infinitely more eager to embrace specific causation here than are fully credentialed members of the scientific community. The pool of "scientists" is never identified (and an endocrinologist, frankly, knows no more about climate than an engineer); the occasion of the "ninety-eight percent" plebiscite remains sketchy, presumably being a stream of voluntary responses to some unpublished electronic survey; and the admonition of truly qualified researchers like Paul Driessen, Wolfgang Thüne, and Wei-Hock Soon is popularly rated alongside the outcry of television celebrities... at which level, of course, the more qualified voices are drowned out.

The climate case, indeed, brilliantly illustrates the nature of the corrosive influence that I have in mind: not science, but "scientism"—the caricature of scientific thinking that has captured the popular imagination. We of the twenty-first century West have a tendency to invoke the holy name of science even as we superstitiously chase Lame Elk from the tribe. "Science" has spoken: there can be no more discussion. Protesters will share in the verdict of exile—or be burned at the stake. The extremely primitive, visceral passion of such cocksureness couldn't possibly be less scientific... but it is dressed in the superficial trappings of science, and its prophecies are elevated at once for adoration. We votaries of the Science God have seen the straight line of events unfolding into the future, and any wandering from that line could prove lethal to progress. Therefore... no meandering allowed.

In a couple of previous books and an online video series, I have discussed the "antinomies of pure reason" that represent what I consider to be the climax of Immanuel Kant's *Critique of Pure Reason*. I won't revisit the subject here in any detail. The gist of the matter is that our human understanding rests upon a logical scaffolding whose foundations would self-annihilate if they were treated as absolutely, ultimately true. The assumptions we make about the beginning of time are perhaps the most readily grasped example of our intellect's essential vulnerability. How did the universe start? There must have been a First Cause, of course: what every schoolchild knows today (or knew as recently as yesterday) as the Big Bang. But of what cause, then, was the Big Bang the effect? Where did the beginning begin? The logical axiom that requires a first cause runs head-on into an equally compelling axiom demanding that any cause be itself the effect of a previous cause. *Nihil ex nihilo*, as ancient and medieval philosophers would say almost in cliché (King Lear flings the phrase at Cordelia): "nothing can be made of nothing."

A much less obvious conceptual collision takes place at the end of time—one which Kant doesn't discuss, and which I myself (as a dwarf who keeps falling from the giant's shoulders) offer with trepidation. It seems to me, however, that "the end of time" makes no sense. If the universe eventually expanded to a point where all motion ceased—where every subatomic particle ceased to pulse, and where the temperature from edge to edge of the cosmos fell to absolute zero—then creation would be plunged into nullity forever. Now, forever is a long time. Infinitely long. Statistically, the odds of our not already being engulfed within that unbounded oblivion rather than mulling over its possibility in our armchairs is zero. Yet here we sit.

One could protest that an oscillating universe would continue to revive forever and ever. This strikes me as a classic case of kicking the can down the future's yellow-brick road (a reflexive act we have already studied in the context of Derrida and the deconstructionists). For oscillation to continue forever, one hundred percent of matter and energy would have to be recaptured at each new firing up of the Bang's furnace: otherwise, though it take ever so long, the pendulum-process would eventually come to a standstill—and the motionless void beyond that standstill, once again, would be infinite.

Enough of this wool-gathering. My intention is merely to demonstrate that our minds do not and cannot *know linear time as an objective condition of reality*. Our minds perceive time in a way that renders it manipulable and allows us to operate somewhat successfully upon our material environment; but the degree to which our metaphysical assumptions about that physical environment are valid cannot be determined—not by intelligences such as ours. We are hemmed in by the very structure of thought that makes us so potent when we consider phenomena within the mind's box. A system cannot assess from within its own confines the degree of abstract perfection in its normal functioning.

One of the many glaring deficiencies in my personal education is chemistry. I didn't fare poorly in the subject; somehow it and I simply managed to steer clear of one another. I was therefore quickly and permanently out of my depth in Stephen Meyer's *Signature in the Cell*. Nevertheless, I fancied that I recognized an old friend when Professor Meyer wrote of how DNA researchers have persistently, even irrationally fought against accepting the "intelligent design" hypothesis of life's origins on earth. The planet isn't old enough—not by a long, long shot—for sufficient chemical reactions to have generated the DNA helix randomly. Yet so wedded is the mainstream scientific community to the notion of life's having evolved haphazardly that new theories tirelessly propose new shortcuts and headstarts. No professional in the book's discussion seriously suggests that alien life forms seeded the earth with already-engineered genetic material from their own arm of the galaxy; but such a claim has been made elsewhere, and it seems to me cut from the same cloth as the equivocations of Meyer's colleagues. Say it were so, and that life from another planet somehow found its way to earth (perhaps by chance on an asteroid rather than in vials transported on a spacecraft). How, then, would DNA have evolved on the planet of origin? The window of necessary time remains vastly too wide for any glass pane fired in our universe's factory to seal.

As I say, this all smacks of Jacques Derrida and his relativist utopian space cadets—of their quixotic self-delusion as they eradicate meaning from the present only to elbow it into the future. Perhaps, after all, the practitioners of "hard science", in their zeal to stand clear of superstition, have indeed ended up substituting one kind of cult for another. For science, be it granted, has no business trying to prove religious faith: it pays its way in the coin of Caesar. (Dr. Meyer never contends otherwise.) There's a difference, nonetheless, between abstaining from explanations about the ultimate cause of things and insisting intransigently that scientific method can find those explanations with more time. No, it can't. Let the scientist not meddle in matters of faith... but let him not claim the authority, either, to "prove scientifically" that faith has no validity.

My days will be linked, one to another, until my chain of worldly time runs out. So for your days, and for everyone's. While we remain on this earth, furthermore, we will understand the seasons as moving in succession, we will think of wars as caused by precedent conditions, and so forth—because, otherwise, we could achieve no understanding of our circumstances adequate to get us from one hour to the next, let alone from day to day. But we do not and cannot know the ultimate truth of time. There is nothing "stupid" or "insane", then, about remaining open to the possibility that the linear sequences of time in which we typically think can only expose fragmentary truths to us. Indeed, it's both rational and even advisable to consider that "true time" may circulate in other motions behind the veil of the time we best comprehend.

CHAPTER TEN

Crosscurrents

Lo bel pianeta che d'amar conforta
faceva tutto rider l'oriente,
velando i Pesci, ch'erano in sua scorta.

The beautiful planet inclining men to love
transfigured all the eastern sky into a smile,
the glow veiling her escort, Pisces, from above.
Dante's *Purgatorio*

I intend for this final chapter of the book's first part to summarize by compacting several assertions made about the "numinous moment" or "event outside of time". Yet before I attempt that act of stitching together, an analogy may be helpful. I've been racking my brain for an adequate one—for a parable, almost, that could convey to our linear-thinking minds how *real* time might match up to time as we know it. I at last came up with something akin to Plato's Allegory of the Cave.

Imagine that you are walking across fog-strewn terrain toward a vague but steady light source. You really have nowhere else to go that offers any apparent sense of destination; for the mist curls so thickly about your feet that you can't even see your shoes, and that shimmering beacon on your horizon is your single reference in the soupy haze.

Unrevealed to you, then, in any discernible manner is the enormous but very gradual staircase across which you walk. Its steps are suited to a giant's feet, each being perhaps three yards wide; yet despite their great breadth, they rise by only an inch at a time. You're actually cutting across these stairs at a broad angle. The result is that you can advance for fifty or sixty yards along one step before you stumble into the next one's rise. Naturally, since you can't see your feet, you conclude at every mild stumble that the ground beneath you is a bit uneven. You have no notion of slowly ascending a great staircase rather than moving ever forward toward the light which—you hope—will be the refuge liberating you from the milling gloom.

Those stairs that come at your progress laterally and throw it off balance once in a while are, of course, meant to represent the "outside of time" moments that subtly take us by surprise once in a while... and then, usually, are forgotten at once, since we assume that our attention should be fixed on forward motion. The biblical phrase "stumbling block" had a part in helping me weave this strange analogy, for we indeed tend to treat such moments as interruptions or distractions. We dismiss them with whatever explanation is ready at hand and get back to the serious business of "progress". Yet what could be more serious, in a spiritual sense, than climbing the giant's staircase and seeing where it takes us? If only we knew that it was there beneath the haze—that the little trips occasionally throwing us off stride all have an order, a higher destination! But our senses aren't equipped to provide such information directly. Any knowledge of the stairs would have to be pieced together with extreme patience, most of it requiring a certain amount of *inattention* to that forward motion we think so full of promise.

For what kinds of experience, exactly, should we keep an eye peeled? In the course of Part One's ramble, I believe I have volunteered three at various points. The first would be personal experiences that have stubbornly stayed with us for years, many (perhaps most) of them deeply rooted in childhood. In discussing the sort of encounter that I myself recall as having knocked me off my stride and stood me upright, I did not mention anything as numinous as an angelic visitation, a message delivered in God's voice, or a Near-Death Experience. That's because I have never lived through any event of the kind. I suppose that those of us to whom God does not speak plain English in a deep, unmistakable voice have a little trouble fully believing those who claim to have been so contacted. We don't necessarily disbelieve them... but we wonder if their personality may be of a naive and very excitable type. Everybody has dreams, and some of us have vivid dreams. (Here I may include myself: my dreams are always in color and sometimes more "high-def" than any waking experience.) A stable person understands, though, that you take a dream with a grain of salt.

Near-Death Experiences I find to be far more intriguing. No doubt, some people massage a rough stay in the hospital until it looks like a trip to the Beyond, just as some people innocently mistake an escaped balloon that catches the sun's last light for a UFO. When so many witnesses of sound mind and solid character, however, testify so resonantly to the presence of something that greeted them as their vital signs flat-lined, I can't wave their words aside. (For that matter, a seasoned pilot makes a very good UFO witness—and there are several such reporters of strange aircraft.) In attempting to recall a book I'd lately read for citation here, I found the author—a medical doctor whose name (Jeffrey Long) at first eluded me—buried on the Internet under a mass of similar professionals. Together, this deluge of credible testimony has thoroughly documented the NDE over the past forty years. Take your pick of the witnesses. It's a pretty impressive list, however you arrange it.

But, no, I have presented in my discussion no such mind-boggling evidence. The encounters I tried to describe do not grab you by the lapels, shake you, and announce sonorously, "I come from the other world!" The most dazzling thing one can say of them is that they simply don't fit into the routine... and they fail to fit in after a fashion that you can't forget, because it so insistently *seems to mean something*. Just what it may mean, you never manage to decide satisfactorily. It's there, sticking out... and you can't smooth it away as the reasonable effect of some handy nearby cause.

Which brings me to a second kind of experience, and a clearly related kind: art. If I had to define an art object (or if I were given the chance to do so—for this is my wheelhouse), I should start by saying succinctly that it "expresses the inexpressible". Then I should probably try to express myself better and end up making a mess of my definition... because the paradox here is ineradicable. A work of art assembles material impressions in such a way as to leave you convinced that their collaboration encodes a vital message, a whole greater than the sum of its parts. You proceed to write an article or a book about the work, if you're a scholar—and the more words you weave together in trying to nab the message, the more fish slip through your net. What we academic types always seem to miss about art is its most fundamental characteristic: that it forever points to something *not quite there*.

Art, I'm convinced, is an angel that God sends to all of us. The winged visitor might be a painting, a temple, or a mere tune—or the simple-seeming lyrics of the tune; but whatever his specific shape, the cherub manages to whack us lovingly upside the head and make us stumble a little on the invisible step of the giant's staircase. All true art calls us to faith. It does so just by nudging us out of our determined forward stride for an instant. Its subject by no means has to be the Crucifixion, the Resurrection, or anything related to any item of orthodox belief. When I was an officer in a regional division of the Conference on Christianity and Literature, a lot of paper- and article-submissions passed under my eye—and the vast majority addressed some issue in the work of T.S. Eliot, C.S. Lewis, Flannery O'Connor, or some other overtly Christian writer. I always regretted such narrowness of focus in our undertaking. I wish we could have faced the academy head-on with the confident assertion that all true art comes from God.

For the academy needed a good stiff slap in the face—or punch in the nose—from those of us whom the angel had smacked... but we instead huddled around "our" authors who, for the most part, had been banished from contemporary college classes, anyway. As I described in an earlier chapter (and will not reiterate now), our ailing culture's intelligentsia have exploited the free pass we gave them to dismantle art entirely, presenting its essential mystery as no more than a cheap kind of hypnotism practiced by the powerful upon the oppressed. That thick-headed, empty-souled program of demoralization should never have been allowed to pass unchallenged.

But it was... and so, as a culture, I think our sense of the mystical lurking in material things all around us has taken refuge in nature. Again, the overlap with other kinds of numinous experience is obvious. Many of my personal "outside of time" moments involved a particular natural setting, and many of the arts draw heavily upon nature, as well. In their quasi-scientific zeal to explain everything away in some "sensible" deterministic fashion, our intellectuals like to attribute our visceral bond with nature to a genetically hardwired "life on the primal savanna" response. *Of course* we love trees! They represented safety from lions when we were naked apes. *Of course* we love purling streams! Every living creature needs water, and water that runs swiftly is least apt to cause illness.

You can hardly win at this game if you protest, "No, it's not the tree's height and the stoutness of its limbs for climbing that I love. It's the intricate play of shadows in the pine needles—it's the soughing of the branches in a breeze." What do you know? You don't have a Ph.D.!

One of the responses that most fascinates me is the one we register to distant sounds: a far-off train whistle or dog's bark, for instance. Perceptions ordinarily registered as "racket" can induce a deep sense of peace when, a mile or two away, they are scarcely heard. Isn't that because of their delightful (yet painful—delightfully painful) hint that even the most energetic spurts of life are but bursting bubbles on a vast ocean's surface? The abyss of meaning here is grandly unfathomable. And how on earth would the evolutionary biologist disarm such a spiritual phenomenon? Would he say that our ape-like ancestors *of course* perked up when they heard distant sounds, because those were warnings of approaching predators? But the approach of a predator would ignite an impulsive fear, not stir up a leisurely meditation—and to argue that the reaction has evolved as we have become less susceptible to predators might explain a diminution of fear, but couldn't conceivably explain the emergence of pleasure. Why can our "best and brightest" not accept that their explanations won't reach every nook of the forest?

I will wander off target again if I don't take care... but I might point out, in passing, that even we non-scientists are now sabotaging our relationships with nature through intrusions of progressive thinking—through cultic outbursts of "future-worship". We can't simply let the indefinite play of light and shadow in a forest or down a mountain glen speak to us of the unspeakable: we have to bend that moment into "activism". We must "save nature" by outlawing the removal of underbrush and deadwood, by replacing mines with the "renewable energy" of wind turbines. In the process, we create tinderboxes that will incinerate millions of acres in the next wildfire, and we erect killing machines that slaughter hawks and other high-flying species by the tens of millions annually... but we sleep better at night, because we have come home from our nature hike with a "mission".

I'm no fan of the internal combustion engine. I recall dropping a word or two about my long walking tours in Ireland and Scotland, and I routinely walked to and from work before my retirement. I'm not out of sympathy with the general distaste for our high-tech pace of living—not at all. But, please... let nature live! Don't be the doctor who starts cutting out organs when a little bed-rest would cure the patient. After putting up bluebird houses around our property, my wife and I have seen families of bluebirds a dozen strong congregate around the watering dish almost daily this past winter. It's a good feeling. We don't really have to go beyond that and agitate to increase the percentage of ethanol in gasoline—which will cause yet more meadowland to be put under the plow, which will destroy yet more wildlife habitat. Every experience of nature doesn't have to feed into a political agenda... does it?

To the extent that it does, or that we let it do so, we seal off what may be perhaps our decaying culture's final portal upon the numinous. I have come to adopt a single word in my thoughts for the ungainly phrase, "numinous experiences", which I shall begin using from here on out. I call these "outside of time" encounters, or smacks in the side of the head, or glimpses out the train's window, or nudges off the tunnel's track... I call them *crosscurrents*. We need to yield to these rare transverse currents whenever they briefly stroke us: we need *not* to attempt to wrestle them onto a vector that parallels our forward motion. They won't go there. They are all telling us the same thing, and it is this. "The purpose of what you do is not the purpose you offer when explaining what you do." Our actions are indeed purposive, if we are good people—but not purposive in any sense that we can define, since their ultimate objective is not of this world. When we nevertheless succeed in reducing our explanations and definitions to terms that make complete sense in this world—and when we thereafter adjust our actions to suit the verbal formulas we have produced in mutilating efficiency—we become less good. We lose touch with the spirit. We skew our forward motion so that we no longer trip over the occasional, invisible step of the giant's staircase. We proceed, instead, along a perfectly flat surface, paying attention only to its "corrected" smoothness that permits a speedier advance... and we climb the staircase no farther, nor do we even notice that we're straying from the beacon at our lower level.

PART TWO

Practical Implications

CHAPTER ELEVEN

Right Here, Right Now

Take therefore no thought for the morrow: for the morrow shall take
thought for the things of itself. Sufficient unto the day is the evil thereof.
Matthew 6.34

I would understand if a reader, having struggled with the abstract notion of "crosscurrents", concluded that an ensuing section about "practical applications" must consist of some pretty far stretches, as well. Applying to daily life a rather eccentric reorientation to time is bound to produce... what? Bowls of milk for restless ghosts or shots of whiskey for passing leprechauns? Yes, I would understand such skepticism.

But the truth is that the wildest flights of fancy we see buzzing about our heads in everyday living are owed to the progressivist, future-worshiping frame of mind. They are authored, that is, by people who won't look at what's right in front of them—who prefer to act here and now as though they had arrived at a peak on the far horizon. When Thales tumbled into the ditch one night as he gazed at the stars, he was at least tracking Sirius and Aldebaran and the rest in their proper sphere. Our futuristic space cadet, in contrast, is trying to immerse himself in situations that exist nowhere but in his imagination. He's likely not just to fall and bruise a knee, but to upset a lot of valuable and long-standing structures around him as he topples.

I can sum up the practical side of resisting the tunnel and being alert to crosscurrents in four words: "right here, right now" (well, two words and a third one repeated). I will offer in the few chapters that follow particular cases of how attention to immediate detail in our encounters makes our actions more responsible. From the outset, I will say that I consider this position self-evident. Does it need explaining?

If so, then the cliché of the lovable grandmother waiting to cross the street may serve in illustration. Her thick glasses indicate that she is nearsighted, and the small parcel she's carrying seems all she can possibly manage. You offer to help her negotiate the traffic: she accepts gratefully. Excellent! You responded to the circumstances immediately before you. In the wake of that do-gooder warm glow, you decide to become the roving defender of traffic-challenged octogenarians everywhere. The next recipient of your chivalrous attention, however, isn't at all appreciative. She is convinced that you have designs upon her parcel. And the next, as well: she prides herself on being "young for her age", and the suggestion that she may need help to do something as simple as crossing the street insults her. Now you're one for three in the do-gooder department.

Your error was to extrapolate the circumstances of a specific success to other cases where they didn't narrowly apply. You formed a general rule of behavior in which "old lady", "diminished physical capacity", and other potentially unflattering factors were knocking around, and you gave insufficient thought to how these factors might upset particular people. Your approach was "one size fits all". By transferring an initially kind and helpful behavior in the present moment to an inflexible routine occupying the future, you nailed down the needle of your moral compass.

Such attempts to put, not just ourselves, but vast numbers of our fellow beings on moral autopilot are epidemic today. Entire nations pass sweeping laws governing minuscule matters of individual behavior. Cities and states within nations respond in defiance, blaring, "Oh, no! We have decreed that all within our borders will act this way and not that way!" From the other direction, nations aspiring to become superpowers pressure rival nations, economically and even militarily, to organize their citizens' lives thus-and-so. The notion that we should have relatively free-floating political islands of permitted behavior—some where all drugs are legal, some where marriage must satisfy certain traditional strictures, some where nobody may own a gun, some where everyone must go armed—is dismissed by all without a hearing. If even such pocket-tyrannies (sometimes called "crucibles of democracy") are unacceptable to the megalomaniac visionaries among us, how much more so must be the generous "live and let live" communities once cultivated by classical liberalism. This is essentially Karl Popper's libertarian model in *The Open Society and Its Enemies*... and Popper's book, I find, has very nearly disappeared. Rare copies are exorbitantly expensive (whether because mainstream publishers have put out an "ideological hit" on it or because the author couldn't be persuaded to pare down his voluminous footnotes... who knows?). To add insult to injury, the freedom-friendly phrase "open society" has been lately hijacked by the most cynical totalitarian on the planet... but no more of that.

We want *big* answers to all our existential problems now: answers stretching far into the future—answers so rigidly rehearsed that everybody will know "the right thing to do" without thinking. That formula, of course, is a moral contradiction (since moral behavior must be freely chosen)... but we don't care. In our utopia of the future, we have decided, everybody will do the predetermined right thing and harmony will be universal. If the human race must be reduced to robotic uniformity in order to reach such a glorious goal and the harmony turns out to be no more complex than a toddler's nursery rhyme, so be it. If dissenters have to die...so be it.

What a fearful world is that one in prospect: what a *dystopia*! That I may sustain my focus on the individual's spirituality, though, let me emphasize two failures of "future-indexed" thinking that compromise the goodness of our daily acts. We've already had a glimpse at both, but I wish to make them explicit.

The first failure is that deeds possibly well meant in crude conception or in their original scene of execution become programmatic. They are no longer decisions resulting from conscientious soul-searching: they are boxes to be checked, a role played by a character cast as "virtuous". Helping Granny across the street is only considerate if it is considered. Dropping a bill into a box marked "charitable contributions" is sometimes an action less reflective than reflexive; and in some regrettable cases, exploiting this reflex may be the source of a lucrative scam that promotes criminal behavior.

The second failure is that the recipient of the good deed is just as apt to become a caricature—a "stereotype", in pop-cultural parlance— as is the deed's performer. We observed this, too, in the case of the "old lady crossing the street". Not every elderly woman wants to be perceived as halting of judgment and unsteady on her feet. Not every person with a Cherokee bloodline, likewise, wants to hear, "Oh, you're part Native American? Well, you qualify for admission under our diversity program." Perhaps the applicant would prefer to qualify under criteria related directly to institutional performance; perhaps he or she does not see that a distant ancestor's ordeal on the Trail of Tears should be viewed as having sent crippling consequences through six or eight generations. Perhaps being a "token" whose handling with kid gloves makes the handler feel better and cleaner does not appeal to every eligible party.

Attention to immediate circumstances in our behavior, contrastively, keeps the burden of active thought upon our shoulders. We are forced to evaluate each case as unique. We cannot put our humanity on "cruise-control". The burden may seem heavy, while casting our eyes far up the road relieves us of having to stay alert to paws or wings that happen to bolt in front of our vehicle. We could very nearly doze off, if only we could settle our gaze on the far horizon... but, of course, people die when you doze off behind the wheel.

Finally, I would stress that attention to life's "irrelevant" crosscurrents recommends that we preserve the past as well as attend the present. This is often a matter simply of understanding context or having perspective—of appreciating that the present doesn't just smack us in the face from nowhere with an utterly alien impact, as if the sky were suddenly to turn orange while the Great Gong boomed from the zenith. Immediate perception depends somewhat upon prior perceptions. Even in dreams, a magical, almost prophetic immediacy grips us most likely because something or someone we'd long thought about in one context when awake bursts upon us in a wholly new context... but we fully recognize that thing or person. Likewise, the waking moments when we become particularly aware of God's "presence in the present" almost always depend upon the occurrence's context being rich with significance. My ethereal moment trudging up a lonely Highland glen wouldn't have possessed the same power if I hadn't been walking all day long—if, say, a bus had just dropped me off and then disappeared.

Now, a child has virtually no sense of the past, yet I have suggested that children are particularly susceptible to the magical present. Precisely because this is so, I believe adults may need to grow increasingly mindful of the past if they are not to be desensitized to the present's epiphanies, dismissing every stunning instant as an "outrider" that—statistically—isn't really happening. Those "orange sky" bursts of surprise at ordinary reality belong to the young child's blank slate. We can't expect to tap into them readily as we age. Our best bet for detecting a crosscurrent, rather, is to cultivate a clear sense of the ordinary's boundaries so that the extraordinary, when it appears, doesn't brush past us unremarked. You won't marvel at the uncommon silence of a mountaintop unless you recollect how noisy the city was a couple of days earlier.

Any profound appreciation of art, obviously, demands a contextual understanding of the work's genre and physical parameters. You can't grasp the mastery of a great portrait or architectural design if you have your nose thrust up against it: you need to have learned where to stand, how to observe, what lighting to seek out. Likewise, you usually can't register the full impact of another culture's art until you've been exposed to dozens or hundreds of examples. First-time exposure even to classic creations within one's own culture can produce more head-scratching than oohing and aahing. The game has rules, and you need to know them before you realize how they're being ingeniously bent.

But I'm not talking about art alone, or even primarily. We all know how parents love the crayon "masterpieces" of their toddlers. A parent who might put such a sketch in a thousand-dollar frame or insist that the local museum's curator consider it for display would be disturbing... but most parents are not of this sort. They fully grasp that a crayon sketch is a paltry thing—and even to them, its magic doesn't consist of its artistic qualities. What they see, instead, is a young mind and a young soul struggling to break into the broader world like a bud struggling to become a leaf. They applaud the effort represented in the drawing, hug the child, and find a spot on the bedroom dresser for the "art work". The real work of wonder is the child who guided the crayon.

We adults have sufficient context to understand as much. When we have an exchange like this with our own child, or when we eavesdrop upon any such event between a young child and a caring parent, we are (hopefully—unless the tunnel has sucked us too far in) nudged by a very mild crosscurrent. We perceive in the moment something that isn't momentary. We feel a bit of God's presence in the present.

It's dismaying to me that so many parents, though—still just a few, but a rising number—may undertake to critique some such trivial creative work and advise the child that, by doing better, he or she will achieve more "success" in the world. The self-sacrificial context of civilized parenting is gone in these cases. The race down the tunnel has already begun; and the window upon the moment's full meaning is closing, not just for these miserable adults, but for the impressionable souls in their care.

CHAPTER TWELVE

Charity: Generous Spirit vs. Efficient Machine

And now abideth faith, hope, charity, these three; but the greatest of these is charity.
1 Corinthians 13.13

I could begin a survey of "right here, right now" thinking applied to specific behaviors from almost any angle, and my survey could also embrace dozens of particular practices. I have chosen to narrow the field down to four behaviors very widely discussed in the context of faith. Furthermore, I'm starting with "charity" (and I'll explain the quotation marks momentarily) because it is universally recognized as a duty incumbent upon the faithful, and also because the ruinous effects of mistaken charity are painfully evident among us. Journalist Diana West has scrupulously detailed in a recent book (*American Betrayal*) how our nation's Lend-Lease program effectively gave Joseph Stalin everything he needed—free of charge—to oppress his own people, subjugate Eastern Europe, and support Mao Tse-tung's rise to power... all in the name of generosity, of fighting against Hitler for freedom and lasting peace! One hundred million murders later (and counting), one has to wish that Franklin Roosevelt's arms had opened somewhat less widely to the golden prospect of a future terrestrial paradise.

Well... let's start with one word. It is very revealing, I think, that "charity" is used today as a kind of reproach (viz., "I don't want your *charity!*"). The reason for that stems from the charitable gift's being viewed as a handout bestowed by a social superior upon his inferior; and the thinking behind *that* prickles with indignation because our grandee is said to perch upon his mountain of wealth, in the first place, due to his success at cheating and bullying his fellow human beings. The tarnished ideal of charity, then, strikes us as flowing from a feudal system long condemned by the greater fairness of our egalitarian world. The needy have a *right* to what we're pleased to call our donations. We should really see our generosity more as reparation.

The entire mechanism of spiritual giving, in other words, has become toxically gummed up with an ideology of envy and resentment. Material success is equivalent to theft. Prosperity is a sure sign of

74

moral turpitude. How did we get here? May one not pay for Tiny Tim's medical procedure, not as a baron would throw table scraps to his dogs, but as a father would look after his own child? Does love, then, not exist?

In fact, Paul's original word as rendered in the Greek New Testament is *agape*, usually translated as "love" and often glossed by commentators as selfless or self-sacrificial love. The English of the King James Bible borrowed from Saint Jerome's Latin vulgate and gave us "charity", from *caritas*. I wouldn't call that substitution a blunder, considering what a mess our language has made of the simple word "love"! No, the problem is that we have perverted the sense of the word "charity"— not that the sense of the word "love" is perfectly clear and should have been preferred.

It's easy enough, in our future-turning, tunnel-thinking society, to understand how the perversion occurred. So I want to fund Tiny Tim's surgical procedure, even though he's no relation of mine... good for me! But what about all the other Tiny Tims in the world? They don't have any such benefactor. Is it fair that a Tim here and a Tim there should grow up to walk straight, while all the hundreds or thousands of others should crawl to an early grave in their tragically crumpled bodies? Of course not! The only acceptable solution can be to provide state-of-the-art medical care to all Tinies everywhere... and anyone who says otherwise is cheating these children of their future. Everyone has a right to the maximum of medical attention.

If you're not already glimpsing certain flaws in this emerging system—flaws far more debilitating than little Tim's crooked spine— then you must be incredibly inexperienced in the ways of the world. In the first place, administering to every affected person around the globe a treatment fully endowed with cutting-edge drugs and technology is a physical impossibility in most cases. The treatment will almost always be either too costly or the number of sufferers too great... or both. Some sort of triage will be required: some sufferers will find relief and some will continue to suffer. This is all assuming, by the way, that the administrative mechanism delivering the treatment is punctiliously honest and efficient.

It won't be either of these. With so much money changing hands and so much at stake, various petty officials along the way are sure to pocket millions of loose dollars, and various concerned parents are sure to submit bribes with the last dime they can scrape up. Bureaucratic labyrinths also simply don't run well. Miscommunication takes place.

Overload occurs. Incompetence often derails operations at least as fearfully as deliberate sabotage. A complex chain is only as strong as its weakest link; and the more links you have, the greater the probability of catastrophic weakness.

All of these links, please notice, have to be paid. One of the ways to ensure against incompetence is to attract professional employees with high wages. But this means that the funds remaining to deliver actual medical services are reduced. Very rapidly, the "fairness" question becomes not how to cure every last Tiny Tim, but what manner of inferior treatment can *fairly* be offered to every patient while none *unfairly* receives the genuine cure.

And I've only looked at the brighter side of the issue so far; even the over-charges raked off the top and the bribes extorted from the bottom are relatively minor corruptions of the system. The real darkness descends when we realize what vast demoralization and venomous resentment arises among the masses. No longer trusting the system, people will lend an ear to any demagogue who tells them how badly they're being cheated and points his finger at a particular group of hoodlums (invariably the same group that keeps him from greater political power). Cynicism runs thick. Average citizens admit petty larceny and intimidation into their own habits because they're convinced that society's leaders practice it on a much grander scale. ("The big thieves are arresting the little one," once quipped that granddaddy of all cynics, Diogenes.) We also find, without fail, that con artists figure out ways to impersonate Tiny Tim and receive a check in the mail themselves. Then we have the samples of social dead weight who magnify their hangnails and headaches, refusing to do any work and clamoring that their "disease" is being prejudicially ignored because the "Tim lobby" has a louder voice.

How is your voyage to Tomorrow's Utopia looking now? As you draw closer and closer to the golden planet, you have to start wondering if, like Venus, your destination possesses an atmosphere whose lovely cast is secreted by swirling poisons.

When we concern ourselves about everyone all at once—everyone to come as well as everyone in the world right now—we must always end up designing a system that reduces human beings to cooperative little machines serving the Great Machine. Nothing else will work. And if you consider dehumanization to be the supreme achievement of charity, then you may as well say that the kindest treatment for any misery among us is swift, painless execution.

The alternative is living in present reality and responding to circumstances immediately before you. In my professional life, I was occasionally approached by a student whom I knew to be gifted and hard-working—and who would thrust a withdrawal slip before me with the explanation that he or she just couldn't pay the bills. Though I was at the bottom of the pay scale myself (a feat I managed to accomplish pretty much throughout my career), I always had enough in the bank to offer help. That's because my family lived frugally—but also because I didn't make such offers to everyone claiming to be in distress. Some kids don't really need to be enrolled in college at nineteen: some of them need to adjust their lifestyle before they address their overdrawn account. Thanks to my knowledge of the specifics, I could offer help to those who would have profited from it most.

Sometimes the mere offer did the trick. The student might be so shocked that a professor had such confidence in his or her abilities that the old battery was recharged rather than replaced. The needed money was somehow found hiding where it had lain untouched: priorities were reshuffled. Yet we seem to prefer writing checks, don't we? Bestowing upon someone a surge of self-confidence is tough to process as a material gift, since so much of it comes from within the recipient (and, of course, from God). Maybe we don't reckon it at a very high value because, as egotistical beings, we'd rather see our bank account take a small, clear hit than content ourselves with a brightening face. A little twinge (not a big one) of dollars-and-cents pain gives us practical confirmation of our virtue. We sleep better on that pillow of calculable sacrifice.

Charity, however, should not primarily be about the donor's quality of sleep. A person with a specific need should be offered specific help: our right hand should reach directly to that person and that need rather than signaling the left hand, in the same gesture of giving, to unfurl the "generosity" flag or to prepare the Pharisee's trumpet.

And what, after all, may we hope to accomplish with any material gift in this world that will be better accomplished with massive dollar amounts but inattention to specific effects? Spiritual giving—charity in its original sense—is about animating the spirit at both ends of the gift... isn't it? Socialist George Bernard Shaw once remarked memorably, "I can't talk religion to a man with bodily hunger in his eyes." Yet we see Christians in China, Africa, and elsewhere willingly incurring far greater distress than chronic under-nourishment for the sake of their faith. We will all die in the flesh of something at some point. Curing every disease on earth will only thrust the office of parting us from our body upon some other messenger (perhaps mass rioting when, healthy and well fed, we take to the streets because we all don't have the same video games). For that matter, people with a significant physical handicap of some sort are among the most spiritual—the *best*—human beings I have ever known. Even though we all live under a death sentence, life in a wheelchair or as a dwarf is not in itself that death sentence.

Now, it's beyond question that I, or any normal adult, would feel frustrated sometimes at not being able to extend resources to where they are sorely needed; and at such times, too, it's understandable that we would grumble a little about those who might do much while doing nothing at all. We must also fight (I know that I personally must fight) against a contrary impulse to abstain from generosity when evidence of a grossly abused donation fouls the air.

These are struggles that we wage within ourselves. They are ineradicable from the human condition. It may well be that whatever success we have in battling through them sets the scene for a crosscurrent—a moment that lifts us outside the flow of linear time. To that extent, perhaps we who bestow charity really do profit from it more than those who receive it.

So uplifting are those selfless moments of sharing that I find in them, alas, one of the major spiritual snares of our time. We "virtue-signal" by giving—and even more by supporting public programs of lavishly generous giving (a strategy which relieves our pocketbook of heavy-duty service). We leap aboard the starship to a better future. We militate for more and more intrusion into farther and farther points of tension on the globe, and we sweep aside in contempt any feeble warning that our ill-informed crusades may be making bad situations worse. Money poured into relief organizations that claim to be filtering food and water to war-torn areas ends up in the pockets of the very tyrants and butchers tormenting the populace. Perhaps donated goods are confiscated and resold at exorbitant prices, or perhaps they are distributed to one side and not the other of a civil conflict. Either way, we might as well have been buying ammo for the tyrant's troops.

But we don't want to hear that. We stop our ears. We cuddle the receipts for our charitable donations tightly to us and curl up in the sweet sleep of righteous justification. Responding to need in a present-

and-personal way is so arduous—and so inefficient, if the world is ever to be purged of all need everywhere!

This is my message. Not only do we *not* draw the spirit more actively into our daily lives by pursuing such manmade perfection; we chase the spirit—harass and hound it—from the face of the earth as our God-substitute machine develops more gears and cogs.

CHAPTER THIRTEEN

Justice: Equality Under the Law vs. Legislated Equality

And one of them, named Caiaphas, being the high priest that same year, said unto them, "Ye know nothing at all, nor consider that it is expedient for us, that one man should die for the people, and that the whole nation perish not."   John 11.49-50

At first flush, it seems odd to say that our understanding of justice today closely shadows everything I just wrote about charity. But then, if we substitute "fairness" for "charity" (as we of the postmodern West indeed do—because "charity" is a demeaning word, we claim), and then we turn to justice, we're merely left with the distinction between the *fair* and the just. Don't most of us nowadays consider these two words synonyms? It's only fair that one child should not be born into poverty while another happens to be born into luxury... isn't it? Isn't it *just* that two infants should begin life at the same starting line?

Not really. In fact, this is a deeper dive into the previous chapter's folly. It's impractical thinking that wanders somewhere between the obtuse and the insane. No two individuals anywhere can enter life with equal endowments, let alone an entire generation of an entire society. Some endowments might perhaps be leveled out... a very few. Privately owned books and instruction at home might be forbidden, for instance, and all education ordained to take place only at formal campuses where all students are taught precisely the same lessons. Yet some children are more intelligent than others, and would inevitably leave their classmates behind despite every effort to equalize results. Some are musically gifted, and some tone-deaf. Some of our students would excel at mathematics... and these might be bullied by others who were given big, strong bodies by Providence. We dare not even venture to say that every child has his or her special gift, and that the practical effect of all gifts at last propels everyone to the same finish line at about the same time. The dedicated writer may find no employment whatever (I speak from experience). The exceptional athlete, in contrast, may become a multimillionaire before the age of thirty—yet his deficiency in handling figures well enough to balance a bank account may plunge him into debt long before he retires.

As we know, too, some people are more attractive physically than others. You can't hide that or ignore it. Ravishing females and tall, handsome males do better at job interviews. The former are pushed before the camera at the network Weather Desk even though, in college, they performed rather less well in meteorology than Jill and Jane. Six-foot-two Randall and his killer smile somehow manage to sell more real estate than pudgy Bob and dwarfish Chuck, who both know the market better and work longer hours.

And speaking of markets... you can dispose of all overt competition and give everyone a guaranteed income not responsive to productivity... but some will still use their guaranteed pittance more wisely, have more success attracting new friends, and resist the common cold more often. Life on this earth is unfair if rated by any material standard you care to choose. It just is. There's nothing you or I will ever be able to do about that.

Not unless we turn ourselves and our neighbors into robots—which does indeed seem to be the plan of preference on certain drawing boards. Even then, I doubt that all robots will be programmed to do just the same chores in the same fashion... but they will not *feel* the "unfairness", the inequity, of existence as we do.

Now, we have lost touch with justice in this "fairness" meander, just as the twists and turns of "fairness" led us away from charity in the previous chapter. Justice has nothing directly to do with table-flat equality. The word derives from the Latin *ius*, meaning "law". The word "fairness" stems from *par*, or "equal". "Equal under the law" is a phrase we know well—but it doesn't mean that our laws labor to make us all equal. The idea, rather, is that the dizzyingly diverse array of gifts showered upon us at birth should not be allowed to privilege any of us over others in matters of legal protection or public duty. If the nation drafts young men to serve as soldiers, the rich man's and the poor man's sons should be equally susceptible. If the law imposes penalties upon a person for driving while intoxicated, the heiress should not receive a warning in circumstances where her maid goes to jail for six months. That's justice. The law which protects you protects me, as well. For that reason, you have a duty to obey the law, just as do I; for we can't be equally protected if we do not lie under an equal obligation to obey. If your father is the state's governor and mine a convict serving a life sentence, our protection under the rules formally established by society and our obligation to follow those rules remains exactly the same.

By the same token, justice demands that people not be penalized for having exceptional ability or determination—and to restrain them artificially from reaching the heights to which their gifts and hard work might have carried them is to exact a penalty. Denying a math whiz a better position or higher salary than his finger-counting competitor in a job requiring advanced calculus would be unjust, even though it would level the playing field. If the members of a football team or the participants in a beauty pageant were chosen by public lottery, who would watch either event, and who would prepare to take part in it? The process of selection would be fair, but it would also be grossly unjust.

I, for one, would probably not watch either named event under any circumstances, and I sympathize with those who believe that our society spends too many resources on elevating athletes and beauties to divine status. Doesn't that simply underscore the main point, however? Carping over your neighbor's success in a certain venue, especially when you don't even value what your neighbor does, looks a lot like envy. If he or she is rich and famous on account of being able to warble silly lyrics into a microphone, what's unjust about that? Apparently, the skill is prized by plenty of "party animals" who perhaps have too much money in their pocket. If you come away bitter from that prospect, then it must be because you yourself have a fierce craving for riches and fame. Is that *just* in you? Your neighbor didn't break any laws... but aren't you breaking *moral law* in nursing a grudge because a person with a rather trivial talent, quite irrelevant to basic survival, draws applause every time he or she steps from a car?

Moral law, you know—or what philosophers commonly call "natural law"—must rest at the foundation of every particular law, or else the latter is merely parasitizing the former's authority and deserves to be ignored. You can't make it a law that attractive people must spend equal time courting all eligible candidates across the spectrum of looks. You can't *justly* require that an organization hire an accountant who flunked half his college classes merely because that person belongs to a "protected racial/ethnic minority". Yes, something of the latter sort is often attempted in contemporary society—and it's within the letter of the law if such a law has been duly passed. But that law is also null and void from the perspective of justice. It effectively punishes X for having a relevant, sought-after gift while rewarding Y for having another gift wholly immaterial to the circumstances.

I'm alluding now to the so-called "social justice" movement. The "SJ warrior" insists that it's unjust for a newborn to be Child Number Seven in a poor family while another bundle of joy with the same birthday is the only heir of a financially prosperous couple. But perhaps the latter child's penny-pinching parents denied themselves more children so that they might bestow more luxury upon their one—while the parents of the seven children, for their part, chose a full house over a big house. Who's to say where fairness lies in these cases? I've known of several "poor little rich kids" who spent much of their lives in drug rehab or psychiatric care. The child of a large, financially stressed family has a much better chance of happiness, according to many studies, than his pampered counterpart as long as two parents are at home to tend to the poorer boy's needs—which, unfortunately, is seldom the case these days; but the root problem, you see, isn't family income. What's unjust to the poor child is the all-too-common circumstance of lacking a father. Imposing a stiff yearly fine (a.k.a. a hefty income tax) upon the single-child family neither addresses the specific social malaise here nor generally satisfies the terms of justice in any legal system but a tyrant's.

Our tunnel-thinking progressives are the engineers of such tyranny. They envision a world without poverty... and, in their zeal to reach that lofty summit, they rather absent-mindedly punish those in the present who are not poor. Of course, the definition of poverty is relative. As long as everyone is affluent at the same level, then you've eradicated financial distress—even if the miserable subjects toiling under your yoke eat only one meal a day!

Justice is not only best administered, but *only* administered, on a "right here, right now" basis. We must not clumsily conclude that our penal system, for example, is unjust when we discover that certain inmates have been unjustly imprisoned. Identify the victimized and set them free after straightening out the paperwork. Let justice be served: that's a just system. For, to turn the coin over, a system is not flawlessly just when only one percent of inmates are victims of wrongful conviction: to win that reputation, it must have an active protocol for tending to the one percent. Set them free, with as much application as you would bring to the task if half had been rounded up for peacefully demonstrating against a dictator. Address the abuse before your eyes. Don't commit excess on either side in grandly fraudulent "idealism". Don't release everyone upon society except the "caught red-handed" simply to boast that your system never incarcerates the innocent!

If I now write of contemporary events without contemporary references, pardon the vagueness. I'm bound and determined not to descend into detail... and a word to the wise is sufficient, in any case. Yet I cannot let the following bitter irony slip past without comment. The most "visionary" among our public-policy makers have lately taken to condemning their political adversaries without benefit of any conventional trial—any orderly presentation and review of evidence by both sides—simply because resistance to the progressive vision is seen as violating Lady Justice. Though two or three names may leap to any younger American's mind here, trust my greater years when I write that the practice has been building momentum since I myself was young. Indeed, the paradigm of the Stalinist "show trial" (not to mention the "necktie party" of the Old West) has left an indelible stain on fairly recent history... but we'd supposed ourselves to have turned the page on such blights, hadn't we? Stalin's chief of security, Lavrentiy Beria, is said to have soothed his boss, "Show me the man and I'll find you the crime." Our own elite national security organizations appear to have resuscitated that spirit of ravenous zeal. All too many of our nation's lawmakers have followed suit. The accused is not granted the right to call witnesses or to interrogate those called against him ("He'll only muddy the water!"); false testimony is openly suborned because its truthful analogues are assumed not to have surfaced yet ("Everybody knows he's guilty!"); our children's future is piously invoked as the cost of letting the scoundrel walk free on a technicality (with absence of evidence being a "technicality"). The future, the future, the future... we must safeguard the future, though we disembowel the present in our efforts! These are the new, self-styled angels of justice....

I think not. Over and over again, I've seen people ruined in academe because they weren't "team players", weren't committed to the "institutional vision"... and the "team" decided that winning the game in the final tally justified breaking rule after rule in the middle innings. (You might call it the "Caiaphas approach".) I won't even insist that the victimized were always principled, thoughtful dissenters: some were, some weren't. What's of the essence here is that no person of principle ever collaborates in the conviction of another person on a false charge, or on a possibly true charge never held up for analysis. Justice is no more social than salvation is collective. Souls are saved or lost only one at a time—and justice can be administered only by scrutinizing this one person's case on this one day beneath our one sun.

CHAPTER FOURTEEN

Non-Violence, Pacifism, Quietism: Windows Upon Higher Peace?

> Jesus said unto them, "Verily, verily, I say unto you, before Abraham was,
> I am." Then they took up stones to cast at him; but Jesus hid himself, and
> went out of the temple, going through the midst of them, and so passed by.
> John 8.58-59

In the previous two chapters, I sought not only to define charity and justice with proper rigor, but also to expose the fraudulent relationship advanced so widely nowadays between practicing charity and doing justice: to explain, for instance, how surrendering one's life-savings to the masses "because I cheated them" is, at best, a gesture of misplaced spirituality. (I might have emphasized that it does nothing to elevate the spiritual awareness, either, of those who claim to have been cheated and who greedily sink their clutches into the offered loot.)

The connection between this present chapter and the following one—between complete abstention from violence and universal dispensation of forgiveness—has more substance. In the previous two chapters, we saw that justice is often misidentified with fairness. Since everyone is allowed by natural law to exercise his or her God-given talents, the needy who lack any special gift may face unfair hardship in struggling to prosper but cannot justly be enriched through the criminalization of their brother's exceptional qualities. In the next two cases, though, the resemblance between both designated virtues (if they be so) is real. Both strict pacifism and blanket forgiveness involve an utter indifference to practical circumstance. In both, yielding to or pardoning an aggressor may have fatal consequences. The "saint" presumably realizes this: it's the source of his possible martyrdom. He knows, that is, of the killing power in the thug's gun or knife which he makes no effort to avert. He must also know that, should he refuse to testify against the thug after the police miraculously arrive to save him, showering the would-be killer with "forgiveness" will leave the streets just as dangerous tomorrow... but the "saint" doesn't care. He'd rather die than send a murderer to jail.

The insanity of such abject quietism recommends it to certain pious dispositions, because we know that God's faithful appear fools to the world (or "idiots", like Dostoyevsky's Prince Leo). The pedigree of abstaining from self-defense or from bearing a grudge is further sprinkled with holiness when we reflect that many other virtues also involve abstinence. As a generality, it seems safe to say that giving free rein to surges of impulse (anger, vengefulness, lust, cowardice) is spiritually misguided, while rising above those surges to preserve a state of serenity shows the spirit's dominance over our weak body and its animal motives.

Furthermore—and here my thesis is put squarely on the spot—an act of impulse seems definitively *momentary*. If living in the moment is spiritually superior to living for a future vision as yet unaccomplished in practical reality, then... why, then, wouldn't the spiritual among us be yielding their self-control to impulse all the time? And wouldn't the resulting world be much more of a Hell than the future one toward which the idealist scales? Because then, in our tangle of momentary responses, we would have slaps answered with punches and insults pursued by vengeful designs....

We've been over this ground before; but it's quite treacherous, so perhaps a second passage will prove helpful.

Being fully open to spiritual reality in the present requires that one's heart and mind be engaged as much as possible by one's surroundings (as when creating or perceiving a work of art, for instance). Impulses do just the opposite to us: they seal up most outlets of consciousness. Raw recruits who experience combat for the first time often carry away no memories of the event, or only very blurred ones. Their confused state also exposes them to greater risk. The old Stoic Seneca, sometimes a little verbose and sententious for our taste, seems nevertheless pretty convincing when he argues in his essays *De Ira* against Aristotle's contention that moderate rage is a good thing in battle. On the contrary, insists the Roman: the ecstasy of anger makes your blows less accurate and puts too much energy into them. A well-drilled, cool-headed warrior fares far better.

Notice here that we're not assuming the origin of violence to lie in a moment of pique or in the proverbial dam's burst after several waves of insult. Violence can be used quite sensibly in self-defense. Several of the most widely practiced martial arts consist essentially in the skill of neutralizing an aggressor—but, yes, the neutralization itself demands energy. You don't stand passively and absorb punches and stabs. Yet is even the degree of vigor involved in self-defense wrong when directed at another human being? Christ never did any such thing.

When Peter drew a knife and sliced off the ear of an arresting officer in the Garden of Gethsemane, Jesus chided him and surrendered without lifting a finger.

The Gospel of John vaguely reports another occasion, however (cited in this chapter's banner), when Jewish officials had every intention of stoning the upstart teacher to death. We don't know exactly how Jesus "hid himself". He wasn't ducking behind a curtain or under a table, because he is said to have walked out right through the midst of his aggressors. No, he didn't leave any bloody noses behind him... but he also didn't give himself up passively to be murdered. If such mortals as we could learn the art of turning invisible, it would surely be the ultimate defensive maneuver. That failing, a little jujitsu isn't a bad alternative.

Avoiding a morally just self-defense (i.e., one which hasn't been preceded by any aggression or insult on your part) appears to me, in comparison, to be a spiritually mangled act rooted in the false idealist's tunnel-thinking. It's not cowardice, that utter passivity, because offering one's throat to the knife certainly requires some courage (unless it's a result of terrified paralysis: we're ignoring such cases here). Yet I reject the proposition that complete surrender occupies a higher spiritual plane. One may as well say that catastrophic fasting— refusal to eat for days on end, promptly followed by a new round of refusals after a little food—is deeply spiritual; and if self-starvation is so, then why not suicide? In that case, the James Jones fanatics and the Heaven's Gate crew had the right idea.

In his *Ecclesiastical History*, Eusebius indeed chronicles extreme acts of fasting, forced wakefulness, and so forth among the cells of early Christians that would evolve into monastic orders. Obviously, he and other observers held such self-destructive behavior in high esteem; and there's no doubt that he either magnified the severity and duration of the sacrifices or conveyed exaggerated reports uncritically, because human beings cannot in fact live on a diet of air or go for weeks without sleep. If God has placed us in this world, then He must have intended that we linger here to some end. It seems to me nothing short of impious to curtail our role in the plan by pulling our personal plug. Starving oneself to death is one such act; drinking poison-laced Kool-Aid is another. Refusing to duck under a club aimed at one's head is still another.

I haven't yet mentioned the irresponsibility toward nameless, unnumbered innocents in the broader community who will suffer if a homicidal maniac isn't resisted. So let's say that you freely surrender your life to the killer (for which he may later pay with his own life, by the way, if captured and convicted); then he goes on his bloody way, unimpeded and unreported. His next victim may be a child. Would not that child's death fall somewhat on your head? You paid the ultimate price to bring your golden utopia into being, as you saw it: your fanatical passivity was merely futile and sad at that level. But when children must also pay for your folly, your vision must assume a share of guilt for real-world, "right here, right now" consequences.

I could write much more on this theme, but my objective is to hold my comments in the vicinity of those spiritual experiences or crosscurrents that sometimes enlighten our brief lives on earth. I suppose the willing martyr (as he sees himself) might know a kind of ecstasy in his dying moment, bleeding out on the sidewalk as the thug ransacks his pockets. This doesn't exactly suit the profile I have proposed, however, for a window of magnified life wherein God's presence is so imminent that the world becomes very precious to us. It sounds a lot more like a dash for the exit.

May I note in passing, as well, that the future-worshiping utopians among us often express a very active interest in confiscating everybody's means of self-defense? Their zeal to build the New Jerusalem from manmade brick and mortar doesn't stop at their offering up their own lives freely to the local banditry; they demand that everyone else make the same sacrifice. It's the same deal as we are forced to strike in creating the perfectly charitable state: we can willingly empty out our pockets... or we can do so under threat of fine and prison. As I write these words, a certain state in the Union, lately delivered to utopian-progressive rule, has actually threatened its residents with attack by the National Guard should any resistance be mounted to a massive surrender of firearms. I find the announcement very revealing. In order to forge the brave new world from which all violence has been banished, citizens must give up their one reliable means of repelling sudden violence—or face death at official gunpoint.

Surely you wouldn't say that these devotees of a "brighter future" have embraced serene passivity in their pursuit of a higher spirituality; or, at least, you must admit that the embrace has all the fraternal love of a steel automation's choke-hold!

I cannot imagine that such take-no-prisoners crusaders for "peace" have ever in fact received a ransom letter with a young son's or daughter's ear or finger in it. Many law-abiding Mexican citizens have known this experience. Alejandro Martí never saw his teenaged boy Fernando alive again after doing everything in his power to satisfy the demands of the primates-in-pants who kidnapped him. In Mexico, private ownership of defensive weapons is a severely punished crime. No word yet about just which year of the future should see the arrival of a terrestrial paradise in that nation.

I have been miserably unsuccessful at keeping this chapter free of acerbic sarcasm. The hypocrisy of virtue-signaling "saints" in the matter of categorical non-violence has cost too many innocent lives for my taste. That said, is there any way that responding to vigorous threats with adequate counter-vigor may ever produce a moment of standing nearer to God's presence? The notion seems implausible. Yet I wonder....

In my own mercifully uneventful life, I have never been compelled to stand up directly against deadly force. On a couple of occasions, though, I was present when tornados passed close by, and I was told later that my "calmness" (which may have been complete ignorance of the danger) was helpful. A similar incident occurred on one of my Irish trips, when the ferry from Rosslare to Fishguard encountered very choppy seas. (Landlubber that I am, I was enjoying the ride out on the deck—and there's absolutely no question that my composure was rooted in stupidity this time!) I have to admit that I remember with much pleasure the minuscule role I played in putting others at ease on such occasions. Naturally, I could have done virtually nothing to reduce real peril if the situations had worsened; but if anything were to be done, we could no doubt have recognized and executed it a little better with cool heads.

Does a cop or a soldier have feelings like this when he rescues helpless civilians from the attack of heavily armed murderers? I should think he would! You might say that his feeling would resemble egotistical pride—that he would be full of himself; but I'd say just the opposite. I think the feeling would be a humble one, something he might express in the little prayer, "Thank you, God, for giving me the power to secure these innocent lives. Thank you for working through such a puny creature as I to keep these lives safely in the world."

And what of the minister who would warble to his congregation, women and children included, "Honor our gun-free zone! Let us rush to our Savior with open arms if a tortured, misguided soul should step through the door with our society's tools of evil!" I've known one such "servant of God". I'll take the soldier's moment of higher peace.

CHAPTER FIFTEEN

Forgiveness: From Man to Man Through God

Then came Peter to him, and said, "Lord, how oft shall my brother sin
against me, and I forgive him? Till seven times?" Jesus saith unto him, "I
say not unto thee, until seven times; but, until seventy times seven."
Matthew 18.21-22

During the final year of my career in academe, a new Philosophy professor came on board. He was said to have contributed a chapter to a recently published anthology about forgiveness. I rarely had occasion to speak to the man, but I sensed that I shared some of his interests. As the weeks passed, I discovered that one of my students was enrolled in a Philosophy course with our popular new hire, and I probed the young man with a few questions. Sure enough, forgiveness was a topic that had come up in his class. "And so what's your teacher's verdict about when to forgive?" I asked. The student answered me in a flat tone that somehow didn't create the impression of someone entirely won over. "Always."

Why the hesitation in the answer—and why the suspicion in me that made my question surface, to begin with? Doesn't Christ essentially tell Peter that we should always forgive? What was my colleague doing but repeating the word of the Lord?

I'd like to ask Alejandro Martí how he would have answered... or, come to think of it, if I knew Mr. Martí better than his own brother, I might just ask him, very tentatively, if he could make his peace with the mere life sentence that would be given to Fernando's murderers. (No death penalty in Mexico—which means, if you get life, that you usually cool your heels in jail for a couple of years before a corrupt judge frees you or a corrupt guard leaves your door open.) I hope Alejandro Martí doesn't doze off at night imagining his child's butchers being whittled away slowly, one limb per day, by Genghis Khan. That sort of obsession poisons the soul. Yet I wouldn't blame him at all if he employed hit men in a rival gang to seek out the killers and put a bullet through each of their small brains. That's not a good path to take, either—because who knows if the right murderers will be murdered, and who knows what innocents may get caught in the crossfire? But on the other hand, I can picture Martí thinking to himself, "How many more men must lose their sons as I have lost mine? If these gangs want my money so badly, then they can have it. I'll finance any gang that kills child-killers." In Mexico of our time, after all, the only justice is frontier justice—with vigilantism immensely complicated by layers of dense, thoroughly corrupt bureaucracy.

So, again... what would Jesus say? Does his "seventy times seven" apply to homicidal maniacs who butcher one child after another and have long buried whatever natural compunction they may feel under the spiritual calluses of habit and the moral depressants active in strong drugs? How do you forgive your child's killer when he smirks at you through his cell's bars and whispers, "Our cartel's *abogado* will get this charge dismissed, and I'll see you out on the streets next month!"

To begin with, the recipient of forgiveness represented by Christ to Peter was clearly a weak soul who repented of his failures yet continued to fail, day after day. I'll bet most of us have a problem of that order: a hitch in our gait that we can't straighten out because of something about how we place our feet. A chronic sin. It may be a matter of over-indulging at the table, or of unleashing humor with too sharp an edge, or of tending to boast whenever we recount an experience. (Sins of the tongue are especially hard to bridle!) I'm pretty sure it is *not* a penchant for kidnapping and gunning down children. "How many child-murders is this for you now, Emilio?" "Oh, I forget... but I'm sure it's not over fifty."

Does that mean that we should not even think about forgiving a kidnapper-murderer? Perhaps he is little more than a child himself— and perhaps, as suggested above, he's so high on mood-altering drugs when "on the job" that he can scarcely remember any victim's face. A couple of points here... Number One: if the criminal sincerely seeks forgiveness, then the offended party must, in return, seek the spiritual power to grant it. How one is to determine sincerity in such a case, I have no very clear idea. The calculation would be the quintessential example of "right here, right now" thinking. If there's no plea bargain depending on a confession... if you can look into the killer's eyes and see something genuine... I just don't know. All would depend upon the particular moment of encounter. Perhaps Mr. Martí could find in his son's killer a not-quite-smothered spark of his son.

Yet forgiveness must be sought of the offended person *through God*: that's the critical foundation of my first point. To grant forgiveness to a man who doesn't seek it—who indeed gives every sign of mocking your generosity, of showing complete readiness to commit the same crime next week—is worse than folly. It's playing God. It's usurping the role of the divine mediator through whom repentance must pass. You are not God. You cannot cleanse a man's polluted soul just by declaring piously, "I forgive you." You don't possess the power of spiritual absolution. You may certainly extend a forgiving hand, and you indeed ought to do so in favorable circumstances. But your hand cannot, all by itself, reach beyond God's doorway into the dark lair where this infected soul gasps. Your palm cannot transmit a fraternal touch to the other's fingers when he holds them stubbornly thrust into a pocket full of gold and bullets.

You may sleep better, to be sure, if you exile the torturing memories of a small, mangled body lying in a casket from your mind and fill your ears with imagined choruses of angels... but spiritual reality, as I've written before, is not about how well you sleep. If your purely self-interested goal is to drive your blood pressure down (and maybe this isn't pure self-interest: maybe you have surviving children to feed), then take a sleeping pill. Get a prescription. But don't use forgiveness as a marijuana-substitute.

In the terms of my small book, dispensing blanket forgiveness round about the wide world with no attention to the offender's penitence is the tunnel-thinking futurism of the progressive. This fanciful fool aspires to bring heaven down to earth through acts of sheer will. "If only I *will* people to be good with all my heart and soul, and if only I treat all of them as if they were completely good, they'll respond! Sooner or later, they'll respond! I will lift them up in my vision! They will rise upon my spiritual magic carpet!"

No... no, what's happening here is that you are desecrating God's creation by disregarding the realities set right before you. We humans are not all good; not a single one of us is ever good all the time. (Even Jesus cryptically responds to one of his questioners who addresses him as "good teacher", "Only the Father is good.") These are the non-negotiable terms of our fallen earthly existence. To ignore them is to attempt to occupy God's throne.

The second point I would stress about forgiving a homicidal criminal is that forgiveness does not constitute legal amnesty. A killer seeks forgiveness on Death Row, not because he hopes to parlay it into a commuted sentence, but because he hopes to die with a clear conscience. Personally, I no longer support the death penalty. (I've seen too many defendants wrongly convicted.) Whatever punishment society decides should be exacted for a heinous crime, however, must be meted out regardless of whether the victim's surviving family has softened toward the perpetrator. The offended party, after all, is also society in general. Justice must be served. We defined justice in the previous chapter. In accord with that definition, individuals must be free to exercise their special gifts. To cut short a life is to suppress such exercise in the most emphatic way possible. Survivors—all survivors in the broader community—must be convinced that the outrage has been recognized and severely punished.

Living within the bounds of immediate reality should teach us of the necessity involved here: people will no longer walk in the park and enjoy God's blue sky and sun if they know that muggers can molest them with impunity. That equation adds up like two and two. Yet our decaying society appears to reject this most basic lesson in justice as it pursues a chimerical notion of forgiveness. Pedestrians who complain that a knife seems to await them around every turn in the sidewalk are imposing their hypocritical bourgeois vision of comfort upon those "free spirits" representing the "other" in the community. Why should you begrudge the contents of your wallet to a homeless man? He needs them more than you do! Not only must you forgive him... you should ask his forgiveness for the coldness you reflexively find in your heart against him!

I would wager that we all recall a moment or two when forgiveness brought a crosscurrent of higher reality into our linear life. Or perhaps the current of forgiving wasn't instantaneous; in my own case, it often comes as a sort of glow overtaking an entire series of unfortunate events. But whether your heart's sublime generosity consumes a moment in clock-time (e.g., forgiving a friend who confesses that she stood by silently as you were slandered) or embraces a span of several weeks or years (e.g., forgiving an abusive parent's behavior rooted—as you now realize—in a very troubled past), the insight lifts you out of the tunnel. You stand above things. You hear a sad, sweet music.

Such a moment is not to be bought at the bargain-basement price of mad fantasy. You don't draw closer to God by showering forgiveness, unbidden and unacknowledged, all around you like a Flower Child at Woodstock bestowing hugs and kisses. Forgiveness is complex: there may be no activity of our hearts in this life which is more so. Christ forgave those who were driving nails into his hands and feet and those who stood about cheering his executioners: he sighed, "They know not what they do." Surely you have learned that people are at no time more deluded than when they follow the crowd. Truly, at those moments, they know not what they do. They ride a current, not from outside the linear flow of life, but from the very mainstream of that flow, rushing ahead like white water bound for a roaring cataract.

We don't know, on the other hand, what Christ would have said about a Roman soldier who (let's imagine) had beaten a Jewish merchant senseless, raped his wife, and then hauled his daughter back to the barracks to be a slave. Or, rather, we know perfectly well what he would have said, and what he would have done. A beast-in-human-form of this kind would have shriveled away beneath the Lord's mere gaze. If the Gospels do not report such horrendous behavior's being displayed before God Incarnate, it's not because things just didn't fall out that way; it's because moral atrocity could no more have occurred in the Divine Presence than a fish can swim in a fire.

Can you picture anyone fool enough, mad enough—fanatical enough—to propose that God's son would have said of these acts, too, "He knows not what he does?" With all due respect to my former colleague (and I do retain much respect for him), moral atrocity is not mere error. It is adoration of the "helter-skelter" (in Charles Manson's phrase, scrawled with the blood of Sharon Tate and her unborn baby) that seeks out and destroys all manifestations of goodness. Righteous indignation, too, can be a divine moment. If you don't know that, then I must wonder if you have known moments of genuine forgiveness.

PART THREE

Paradoxes of Formal Faith

CHAPTER SIXTEEN

"Natural Religion": Revelation Through Heart and Mind

> For the wrath of God is revealed from heaven against all ungodliness and
> unrighteousness of men, who hold the truth in unrighteousness. Because
> that which may be known of God is manifest in them; for God hath shewed
> it unto them. For the invisible things of Him from the creation of the world
> are clearly seen, being understood by the things that are made, even His
> eternal power and Godhead; so that they are without excuse.
>
> Romans 1.18-20

Nothing I wrote in Part One of this book was intended to be dependent upon Christian assumptions... but then, I assume as a Christian that the rudiments of my faith address the realities of basic human nature. Theologians speak of this position as "natural religion". The concept has nothing to do with worship of trees or prayer to the Moon; it implies, rather, that God has inspired all human beings with intimations or "inklings" (as C.S. Lewis and his friends styled them) leading to true faith. Such embedded hints would include, of course, our conscience, and also—in my opinion, often expressed above—the mysterious power that beauty exercises over us. We are made to love God and, to some degree in this fallen world, to know Him. We are made, at any rate, to be dismally unhappy without Him.

As human beings, after all, we share certain qualities and toil under certain conditions: the common ground is quite extensive, really. We live for perhaps four score years, and then we pass from this world. In the process, we stagger toward spiritual maturity through a period of ignorance and confusion which perversely breaks into sunlight just as our physical performance embarks upon a downward slope. The two vectors meet briefly at a peak called the *acme* by the ancient Greeks, our knowledge and understanding somewhat stable at last and our bodily strength and resilience not yet notably diminishing. Naturally, our social relationships (for we are a very social species, though saddled with many an unsociable individual) are complex—and they undergo complex transformation throughout our lives. As adults, we need the guidance of elders most when we are best equipped to wrestle material challenges; and as we become superior advisors, we also become less capable lifters and haulers. Obviously, our childhood transpires in almost utter dependency. A little less clearly (because more dreaded and concealed), we may be reduced in our final years to a second infancy by failing memory and the breakdown of basic anatomical functions. Xenophon had a theory that his teacher Socrates had baited the judges so relentlessly when on trial for his life because he indeed hoped for execution: his greater fear was that the "second childhood" might soon overtake him and reduce him to a babbling fool!

During certain epochs and in certain cultures, we seem especially prone to rebel against one or more of these parameters. We don't want children hampering us—or else we want to remain children ourselves (which may partly explain why we don't want the real item), or we want children around but don't want to rear them. Young people may regard anyone over thirty as fit only for the slaughterhouse, having decided that no one beyond that age could possibly possess any wisdom worth tapping. The aging may concentrate on piling up enough loot to pass their "golden years" in perpetual vacation, providing no benefit to themselves or anyone else beyond infusing a frivolous economy with a steady flow of cash. The old grow senile before their time—and are more hidden than ever, as if the Death's Head once passed around medieval feasts were now a walking horror mounted on bent shoulders.

Of course, I've lapsed into describing our own time, and particularly as we see it in the Western world. Prosperity has brought us the blessing of individuality... but individuality has levied upon us the tax of a radical freedom which few of us are willing to pay. The challenges faced by all reflective human beings of all places and times are magnified in us. We have too much affluence, perhaps: too much mobility, too many amusements, too many sexual options at too low a risk of responsibility, far too many employment and career choices (but with far too little promise of genuine pride in our daily labor). Some of us appear eager to surrender our freedoms wholesale to a perpetual Dutch Uncle or Nagging Auntie—someone who will lift from us the dual burdens of having to choose amid such confusion and the guilt following close on the heels of wrong choices. Just do it for us, please... *someone*!

Yet this, too, has happened before. I'm nothing remotely akin to an Old Testament scholar—but any of us could readily excavate from those ancient texts instances of a fallen people clamoring for a king or idolatrously bending its collective knee to a golden calf of its own fashioning. That's us to a "t". Our here-and-now follows the Old Testament paradigm the way Christmas goodies tumble from a cookie-cutter.

As human beings, we don't have in this life what we ultimately need... or we have it in fragments or see it drift across our path like a misty waif at midday. It doesn't correlate to the rest of our busy schedule, so we brush it aside. Ground clutter on the radar: static interfering with the radio's news flashes. We muddle forward, because the religion of progress tells us that our only possible salvation lies up ahead—and not even a salvation for us personally, but for our race or species (or for some new species to which lab technicians will "upgrade" ours). We do a pretty good job of keeping that line pointed stiffly straight. Our skill at scouting out the abyss into which it leads is less impressive.

Nothing we do along the way, at any rate, gives a sense of fulfillment for more than a few days or weeks. Our riches buy more luxury, more amusements; but the feverish activity that produces such wealth leaves us little leisure to enjoy its purchases. Or if we are wise enough (and this does indeed represent a kind of wisdom) to desist from a no-longer-necessary servitude to the dollar and spend a few coins from our pile, we find that the amusements are but ritual repetitions of our lifelong struggle refined cleverly into a game. Have we chased the White Stag, then, only to discover that capturing him allows us to sit for hours before a high-def screen playing Chase the White Stag on video?

Perhaps those who claim to have achieved the greatest fulfillment are those who "live for others", organizing charitable drives to assist flood and hurricane victims, crusading in the courts against laws that oppress minorities, lobbying politicians to alter the circumstances that make child enslavement profitable, and so forth. Excellent causes, one and all... but how many of us pause to consider that relief of misery cannot—in and of itself—be the ultimate end? If it were so, then our fulfillment would disappear as soon as our heroic efforts reached their objective. No, that's not likely to happen in this world! Christ tells us that the poor are always with us... so are we, then, *relieved* to hear that? Do we need the poor more than they need us? Does our happiness depend upon the endurance of their misery? Or, to lay the metaphysical trap from another angle, have we nothing to offer the poor, the oppressed, and the suffering at the end of their dark tunnel except high-def TV's and video games? But was not that materialistic nullity—that vegetative state of passive consumption—the very scourge which drove us to flee into a life of self-sacrifice, in the fist place?

What does it all mean? Must we forever kick the can farther down the future's road, waiting for the return of the Prophet or the arrival of the Kingdom—or engineering some such transformative event out of technology that travels to new star systems? Must we always postpone the final answer to the final question—and must we always kid ourselves that the Answer of Answers itself, if we ever manage to formulate the question, is not another postponement?

Now, such adoration of the future has not, in fact, always represented a fixture in the human condition to the degree that it does among us today. I began this little book by observing that peoples of the past—for the vast majority of our historical record, and probably for all of what extends beyond the historical searchlight—drew far more contentment than we from a sense of cycle. They expected to age and to die. They found a profound comfort in their children and grandchildren—who did not leave them to build individual, independent lives, but who learned of timeless traditions at their feet and constructed a life within those traditions. God forbid that we should lapse back into a mesmerized, uncritical tribalism! But our individualist approach to life in the West (which, properly speaking, is a value system rather than a tradition) constantly runs extreme risk of being caught in the gravity of future-worship. We have virtually no cultural respect whatever for the past to keep our starship from veering into that all-annihilating black hole.

It's my opinion that the Christian faith holds the key to preserving a primary regard for each soul's worth without alienating individuals from a higher destiny intended for all. I have argued that the way lies not in some hazy future whose folds allow us to conceal contradiction, but rather in the present which slips past our eyes largely unseen as we squint into tomorrow. Time is indeed that White Stag in Sorley MacLean's forest. It tears our soul apart in an exhausting chase that never ends in capture... if we let it draw us into the Dark Wood's linear tunnel. But perhaps the Stag would come to us, if only we would stand still and see the whole forest rather than one vanishing tail.

I have organized this final section as a series of paradoxes. Their number is no more exhaustive than was that of the practical implications undertaken by the previous section. (In other words, I could certainly produce a list twenty or thirty items long if I had the wit to compile it and you the patience to read it.) Why such foregrounding of the paradox as a delivery vehicle for religious insight? Because the paradox responds to the "complex simplicity" underlying everything essential to life, as well as I can make out. What I know in my mind and feel in my bones is twofold.

First, our linear conception of time poses a tremendous impediment to faith—and as individualism and the scientific revolution have both promoted this conception in our lives, faith has come to us much more rarely. To a great extent, however, linear thought is natural to us, and utter resistance to it (if even possible) would render us almost as intellectually inept as a vegetable growing on a vine. Some sort of compromise is required. My intent in concluding the book with this section has been to emphasize the climactic quality of finding that compromise—of negotiating a truce with the "tyranny of the line". There's a way out of our spiral of despair. Considering the possibility that a straight cause-and-effect chronology, necessary though it is to our thought, doesn't describe ultimate reality can be delightfully liberating.

A skeptic like me, to be sure, ought to leap up and protest, "Well, just because something's delightful doesn't mean it's real—reality more likely awaits us in just the opposite direction!" I will respond to that caustic criticism in the book's truly concluding remarks. For now, allow me to say simply that a self-deluding flight from reality—in a word, fantasy—is fully distinct from a speculative supplement to reality that better accommodates our natural chemistry. The difference is the same as that between wearing rose-colored glasses and supplying statistically likely details to a satellite image's deficient resolution. Or think of reverse-engineering a mysterious engine. You can try to muscle the strange sprockets and gears into something that satisfies your wildest daydreams... or you can connect the parts spread before you in ways that actually make them click and whirr.

My second point is merely a reiteration of how tightly paradox is woven into our human fabric. Critics of faith, and especially of the Christian faith, can be relied upon to remark that it doesn't "make sense" in some narrow (usually linear) manner. But life itself, as far as we can tell from our unpromising position deep within its box, doesn't make much sense. The highest truths about human life, therefore, would probably express observations about the box itself which we box-dwellers will be sure to find a little crazy. Again, I well understand that a fantasist might make this very claim in defense of his seeing ivory castles in the clouds. The distinction is that such fantasies are not paradoxical, but beautiful—and we can indulge beauty, or even find in it a motive to sense the presence of higher reality (as I myself have argued here)... but the beautiful fantasy remains merely a stimulant to the sense of "beyondness". It does not propose a design, a schematic, for how the Beyond might truly be integrated into the little that we fully understand.

Hence my devotion to paradox. I don't wish to found my faith—or to lure you into founding yours—upon fully imaginable flying stallions and singing stars that we can both fully recognize as fanciful. Such faith is cultic. Let us found our faith, instead, upon a riddle whose answer we are not quite capable of grasping, but whose amplitude benignly explains our fancy's tirelessly flapping wings and the longing in its songs.

CHAPTER SEVENTEEN

The Paradox of Spiritual Rebirth

And they brought unto him also infants, that he would touch them; but
when his disciples saw it, they rebuked them. But Jesus called them unto
him, and said. "Suffer little children to come unto me, and forbid them not;
for of such is the kingdom of God. Verily I say unto you, whoever shall not
receive the kingdom of God as little child shall in no wise enter therein"
Luke 18.15-17

**The believer is asked to accept that the soul is mystically energized in a
"second birth" when the body reaches a certain stage of maturity, or
when the adult learns moral lessons from worldly experience, or when
God—on some timeline that seems wholly arbitrary to us—sparks the
invisible generative event. Yet spiritual birth, or "rebirth", is incoherent
from any of these perspectives.**

The notion of spiritual rebirth hardly seems like an inhibitive
factor to faith. On the contrary, many would say that it is the
foundation of the Christian faith. And even the unbelieving among
us—or even those believers who flinch around denominations styled
"born-again Christians"—all accept the premise that people may
change radically in their moral outlook as they mature. I recall one of
my favorite college professors telling a class of us undergrads that not a
cell in his body remained from the days when he was twenty. Though
his remark was factually incorrect, I took his point.

For the record, the "born again" passage at the beginning of John 3
uses the Greek word *anothen*, which can mean either "again" or—more
literally—"from above". Jesus repeats the word insistently to
Nicodemus; and he caps his explanation with the unforgettable verse
8—"the wind bloweth where it listeth," etc.—that the synoptic Gospels
also report. (By the way, the word *pneuma* is tantalizingly ambiguous,
as well: it can mean either "wind" or "spirit".) One may justly object
that no consequential difference in meaning exists here—that to be
born from above is indeed to be born again. I don't dispute that we
human beings are hard-wired to represent time in our minds as a linear

chronology; I have indeed emphasized the point at several junctures. Yet I find the "from above" footnote worth logging for the additional dimension it brings to a spiritual enigma. I wish to return to that footnote later.

Here at the chapter's outset, let me suggest that—in spite of appearances and presumptions—at least three impediments to profound faith crop up if we apply the "born again" blueprint rigorously to our spiritual conceptions.

1) The necessity of this second birth implies that he who hasn't yet exited the mystical womb must remain dead in spirit. That would include children, who obviously haven't lived long enough to acquire any such experience as would prime a change in their moral horizon (or long enough, in many cases, to have acquired any such a horizon). Most Christian denominations have traditionally skirted the issue by baptizing children before they can utter a word, or perhaps before they can even focus their eyes. The baptismal water, so goes the tenet, is half of the "water and spirit" formula mentioned by Jesus in John. Yet Christ also says, and says rather peremptorily (in a passage offered as this chapter's banner), that we shall not enter the kingdom of heaven unless we become as little children. It seems ironic, if not contradictory, to claim that children must receive a special dispensation for their lack of adulthood in baptism when the Son of God himself says that adults must recover something of their abandoned childhood. The bottom line of linear salvation is that it denies admission to those who die very young and to those, as well, who die before having lived widely enough to discover a Christian tradition alien to their cultural surroundings.

2) If we remain wedded to this inflexible timeline, furthermore, we are forced to believe that the born-again, having once been saved, cannot backslide. In a way, the problem here is complementary to the previous problem: some people don't live long enough for their initiation, and some people live too long—so long that their "old" manner of living contradicts their new birth. I have known cases involving re-commitment (and re-recommitment) at the altar as struggling individuals move like the proverbial yo-yo between sloppy-drunk skirt-chasing and teetotaling tightrope-walking. *Nella chiesa coi santi ed in taverna coi ghiottoni*, quips Dante: "In the church with saints and at the bar with boozers." Hypocrisy, I well know, is as natural to us as breathing air. It's certainly the proper business of no person, believer or non-believer, to sit as

judge over the sincerity of his fellow beings' spiritual life. Nevertheless, as pure doctrine, the born-again paradigm forces us to ignore hypocrisy even at the theoretical level. That is, it shuts us down cold and hard if we attempt to utter the common-sense observation that some people—no names needed, no specific persons targeted—aren't spiritually more alive just because they had one atypically clairvoyant day. The doctrinal gag-order is something akin to the legal foul of suborning perjury. The New Testament, certainly, shows a lively awareness that "once saved always saved" doesn't describe spiritual reality. Romans 8.12-13 and 11.19-22, John's brief second epistle, and many similar passages warn that believers must not grow complacent and assume a special place in God's grace. Yet linear thinking lures us almost into commemorating a particular square on the calendar as our "salvation birthday".

3) The least obvious problem is, to my mind, much the most damaging. It is so transparent as to be nearly invisible. Let me, therefore, try to state it very carefully. If we are spiritually reborn in life, and if the rebirth is not simply a matter of being sprinkled with holy water (a formula with few convinced adherents), then we must suppose that some experience or sequence of experiences has reoriented our value system. We have grown morally. This means that we accept the notion of life's being a kind of guru to us. We are self-centered as children, we carry that focus into adolescence and nurse it into full-blown egotism, we proceed as adults to strut about pompously upon the toes of our fellow beings, and then something happens—a death, a public disgrace, transformative love for a superior individual—to snap our vision around to a farther horizon. Excellent! Except... except that "the world" thinks in precisely such terms. The evolution I've just compressed has nothing distinctly spiritual about it. Bill Gates made incalculable piles of money, some of it (so rumor runs) by ripping off Steve Jobs... and then he morphed into a paragon of civic-mindedness. Warren Buffett, the Koch brothers, Michael Bloomberg, Tom Steyer... all fabulously wealthy, all dedicated in later life (or so their tax returns suggest) to funding charitable endeavors, and none with a word to say on behalf of the spirit. If our message is that "life experience" humbles the proud and awakens Scrooges to the presence of a broader human family, then... then how is our program any different from the utopian pep-rally that gins up support for social progress? "Let's all pull together! I once was lost, but now I'm... a heavy donor to the Green Movement!"

There can be no doubt that life is indeed a great teacher—but it also cannot be the only teacher, or even the primary teacher. If you learn to have more consideration for others because your road was bumpy when your were behaving like a spoiled brat, then you have acquired the practical awareness that you get more of what you want out of people if you give them more of what they want. Sorry... but this isn't a spiritual insight. It's definitive pragmatism: it's heedless selfishness disciplined by selfish calculation. In fact, it's advanced "adult thinking" of which no child is capable. It reflects a heightened sense of the linear "mission"—the "goal-oriented" march toward increased sales, enhanced productivity, heightened popularity, and more extensive influence. With disturbing frequency, such disciples of the guru Experience return from their journey to the mountain monastery pondering a plan to engineer their fellow beings' "progress"—a plan having plenty of carrots and sticks to hurry their neighbors along the revealed path. All humanity will benefit if only the education system is overhauled to do thus-and-so, if only society's energy needs are supplied this way rather than that way, if only births are held at such a level and diets are regulated in a certain way.

In other words, if rebirth is associated with greater wisdom acquired by experience, then the result very commonly tends to be an acceleration down the tunnel of future-idolatry. "I have lived long and learned much," says the sage. "Now I will proceed to give all of you the benefit of the high revelations I have received. Don't question me. You haven't been where I have been, and your understanding is no match for mine."

My personal opinion is that no species of mentality has been more effective in annihilating the spirit from contemporary living than this one. The fallacy here lies in the supposition that our moral compass grows more magnetic as we steep ourselves increasingly in worldly affairs. It doesn't. To say that the moral beacon, rather, tends to dim as one is more immersed in day-to-day exchanges would have greater plausibility. I think that's why Jesus recommends the child as a model for spiritual renewal. Children know virtually nothing of the world... but they seem to have keen sensors in the matter of fraud. They know when the answers they're getting from adults are not addressing the "right here, right now" facts, but are rather trying to sell them on a fake reality which may or may not come to pass if other people can be cajoled into cooperating. "Sure, we'll go on that picnic this Saturday! I just have to get your mother to skip that stupid reunion so that I can work late Friday night." Children can smell out the traps in such equivocation because, while their world is admittedly self-centered, it isn't dedicated to some complex construct of Self standing on a pedestal of accomplishments and glories. Their wants are basic: attention, food, sleep... and more attention. Their young minds are riveted upon the present, and so they quickly notice when the adult mind wanders into the future's haze or into an alternate reality's tissue-thin structures.

Naturally, it's not to a state of severely confined intellectual horizons that Jesus would have the believer reduced. So how, exactly, does one "receive the kingdom of God as a little child" as Christ exhorts us to do in Luke 18.17? I think we've just seen how. Being an adult, one has access to broad and profound moral insights not available to children *but also not taught by experience*. Such insights are not screened or filtered by an adult's egotistical focus on "accomplishments"—on elevating a Tower of Self that shines far and wide. Rather, they preserve the child's concentration on what is right here, right now: peace and beauty, the separation from peace and beauty belonging to the terms of physical existence, the suffering born of that separation, the projection of such yearning and suffering upon every other human creature... none of this has to do with your bank account's size, your level of respect in the community, the volume of parties to which you will be invited, or the degree of ink spilled in praise of your latest book or speech or movie. None of it has to do with a "reality" sustained largely by your imagination. It has to do exclusively and entirely with the present moment—the eternal moment which makes God's reality forever present.

To be born again is to be born from above. It is to recover the child's riveted focus on "real reality"—a focus whose complete mischaracterization has become a cliché among us adults. For to us, children's minds wander: children live in "make-believe". They gaze at sunbeams. They stop everything to listen to a siren or a street-sweeper. They notice that a stack of empty boxes looks like a staircase... and we chuckle at their imagination! Meanwhile, we fail to grasp that our "realist" devotion to pursuing a new job for the sake of affording a bigger house in a "better" neighborhood involves calculations of a far more fanciful nature—for happiness, honestly, looks much less like a manicured lawn than a staircase looks like three boxes.

The rebirth of the spirit, I would submit, is a *coming alive* to the eternal moment with an intensity we possessed as children but whose full significance a child cannot appreciate. As children, we were already alive to that moment… but we didn't know that there were moments of any other sort. As adults, therefore, we face a task of recovery, of excavation—and for some of us, the digging is far more laborious than for others. Some have left what they knew as children very far behind, indeed, as they charged along the adult sequence of objectives reached, missions accomplished. These are the same people who insist that spiritual rebirth involves an utter rejection of the person they used to be. They're likely to tell you that every cell in their body has been replaced since they were twenty.

But not really: not biologically, and not spiritually, either. The "new man" was always there in the child—was indeed older than the "old man", who came along and covered the child up for a while… yet Old Man's predecessor was never old, thanks to being a child. Before Old Man was, Child is.

There's your paradox. We do not have to live a life of a certain length to find God, nor do we have to encounter certain crises in life or be initiated into a certain body of worldly wisdom. We need to become more of what we are, more of what God made us. As children, we were God's beloved, His favorites… but we could not remain children in all ways of the understanding. Hence we struggled to preserve what we had, what we were, even as our horizons broadened and lengthened. We had to remember not to dwell upon our new horizons—to remember that one can dwell only on the earth beneath one's feet.

We don't need a future to complete ourselves. We need, on the contrary, a completion in the eternal present if we are not to be overpowered—seduced, inflated, terrified, maddened, deceived—by the future. What we will be must become more of what He is so that we may recover what we were at birth.

CHAPTER EIGHTEEN

The Paradox of Bodily Decline

Jesus answered, and said unto them, "Ye do err, not knowing the
Scriptures, nor the power of God. For in the resurrection they neither
marry, nor are given in marriage, but are as the angels of God in heaven.
But as touching the resurrection of the dead, have ye not read that which
was spoken unto you by God, saying, 'I am the God of Abraham, and the
God of Isaac, and the God of Jacob?' God is not the God of the dead, but
of the living."   Matthew 22.29-32

**Believers are asked to accept that the soul lives eternally; yet the body in
which this soul is briefly imprisoned for some reason is astonishingly
fragile, often not surviving childhood, never reaching old age without
undergoing a deterioration of vital powers, often ending up in pathetic
collapse wherein little intellectual capacity is observable. Such a shell
gives no sign of housing an immortal occupant.**

There is no paradox here unless one accepts the enduring life of
the soul after the body's death. Otherwise... the body dies, and the
curtain comes down on our personal drama. The rest of the world
won't be far behind. All that has ever lived reaches an end. Indeed, I
discussed early on the lofty despair of the "chronological sublime",
where one actually senses an odd exhilaration in contemplating
something like a vast graveyard, a museum full of dinosaur skeletons,
the dilapidated ruins of an ancient city... prospects that free us from our
minuscule mortal perspective and allow us—briefly—to float above the
whirl of eons.

But who are *we*, at such moments? What is the free-floating "I"?
What identity does our intellect imagine is riding the crest of this
history-dominating wave? Even in trying to conceive of our puniness,
we back into a spiritual realm where our conceiving self, our reflective
or brooding or desperate self, refuses to be defined within the limits of
a sack of guts. The paradox, therefore, urges itself upon any mind that
cannot resist belief (as no honestly thoughtful mind can do). Since all
of our waking activity—and even (or especially) our time spent in
dreaming—tugs us toward shadowy recesses of experience where the

body can scarcely follow, why exactly must we have a dull body holding us back?

For if there really were a substantial reality beyond this one, you'd have to suppose that its ruler—our creator—could have done a lot better in designing a vehicle for our souls: he could at least have given us wings! Instead, we must inhabit these humiliating shells. They can't stay awake for long, their maw needs constant stoking like a damp fire, the byproduct of their fuel consumption is far more repulsive than smoke or soot, and about two thirds of their normal lifespan is spent in a decline that greatly accelerates toward the end. The Greek poet Hesiod wrote that, during the Golden Age, men simply lay down and went into a sleep of death while still fully in their physical prime. If only *we* enjoyed that luxury!

High-tech luminaries like Ray Kurzweil believe that we might indeed enjoy it—that luxury and many others—in the not-too-distant future. All we have to do is fuse our biological conveyance with "upgrades" of an artificial design. Once our circulatory system is injected with millions of microscopic robots ("nanobots"), we will become disease-free. Wounds and fractures will auto-repair overnight. Our supplemented brains will work the most intricate calculations within milliseconds, and the power latent in our muscles will be so effectively tapped that we will leap tall houses (if not tall buildings, like Superman) at a single bound. Most importantly, we will become all but immortal. We may live ten thousand years... and I would imagine that, as our ten millennia are elapsing, our ginned-up brains would devise ways to add another hundred.

Actually, Kurzweil's "paradise" isn't at all a bad entrance into a spiritual appreciation of the bodies we presently have. Picture his brave new world in detail: what aspects of life would disappear, besides death, disease, and injury? Well, let's start with a closer consideration of deathlessness itself. Certain prospects will vanish from your psychic horizon as mortality is lifted from your shoulders. If you don't die, time grows virtually meaningless. There's no pressure to get anything done, to reach any destination. I realize, naturally, that my book is a wide-ranging argument against the "linear tunnel" that draws us chasing after an ever-recessive Shangri-La... but now imagine a reality where no resistance at all to our idolatry of the future would be needed. Any sense of crosscurrent-reality would also vaporize. Tomorrow would have no relevance, and neither would today (let alone yesterday). Rather than seeking after meaning in the mad forward lurch of time, we would be drowning in a meaninglessness of inexhaustible temporal wealth.

Why would certain strains of music give you an exquisite pain, a yearning for the inexpressible? What's pain? What can you not express, you who possess infinite time and almost infinite power to go and get whatever takes your fancy? And without that sense of absence, what presence of temporary or partial joy would you register? Wouldn't you grow bored, rather, with the very moons of Jupiter that you use as balls in a game of galactic billiards? To know that nothing you undertake would ever run up against any practical deadline, and that, therefore, no sense of that which defies all ends could ever illuminate your spirit... where would you be in such a state, if not genuine Hell?

There would be no children, by the way—a detail I stress because nothing has so enriched my own material life on earth as being a father. Why would a creature whose years are measured in eons have a child? With no death to stabilize the population, new life would quickly upset the ecological apple cart. And what pleasure, at any rate, could a being who never ages take in another being born almost instantly into maturity? (Nanobots, of course, would accelerate the new arrival through childhood within days.) The trade-off of multiplying gray hairs for a quickening intelligence in the child's eyes, a deepening gratitude for sacrifices made... no, none of that.

Every reflection would inevitably rotate back upon the self, in the absence of any Father Creator or any child created; and a self, in the absence of restrictions, limitations, parameters... what would that be, exactly? Or approximately? An immense, undifferentiated web of impulses, the whole as fitful and beyond all moral boundary as the gods of darkness and chaos. Feel an urge, fight a war, lose an arm, grow the arm back, trap the victor, rape his queen, forget a scheming minion, be decapitated from behind, grow the head back, grow a second head for good measure... what a nightmare! It sounds like the crudest, most dismal pagan myth imaginable of cosmic origins, produced by a tribe clinging to an active volcano's flank.

Now do you begin to see why the tight corporeal boundaries within which our soul must move may be the perfect growth medium for a healthy spirit? We require a context within which to absorb certain essential truths about reality beyond all context. Linear time is part of the stress placed upon our understanding: in some ways, it seems to be the primary source of stress. We're forced to think—to bestow value and learn subordination. We will die, yet something within us—some breeze that blows lightly through us—passes on. What exactly is that wind which "bloweth where it listeth"? It cannot be a pleasure of the senses, a titillation which we share with lower animals and which dies within instants, making even our frail bodies seem durable by comparison. It isn't *us*, this restless motion, insofar as we are of these bodies... yet our attraction to it works so powerfully that we would eagerly die in its service—and perhaps, then, it is indeed us in some higher sense. Or, at least, we must surely be *of it*.

I mentioned "growth medium" just above as a metaphor—but perhaps a better analogy could be constructed from the notion of "artistic medium". A painter needs canvas and oils. Neither appears a very promising means of representing nature if, as a child, your only experience of design was paper and crayon or colored pencil. Yet there's a technique to it all. The canvas's rough surface captures the oils, which can be massed in clumps to produce amazing effects. I had the good fortune to be able to study a couple of Turners several times at the Kimball Art Museum in Fort Worth as a young man. I would never have imagined, merely from seeing photographs of Turner canvases, that his spectacular sunsets and conflagrations owed so much to bright paint piled into thick clusters or heavily flaked. From viewing the work of relatively mediocre painters, as well, I soon learned that the impression of reflective metal or of leaves in sunshine was not achieved by mixing just the color perceived by the eye—no; it was *the mind assimilating effects through the perceiving eye* that imposed brilliance on the represented object. The painter—any painter of modest skill— would infuse background colors of an appropriate shade with white or nearly white streaks or flecks. The viewer would combine the two unconsciously and see a metallic flash or sunbeams sparkling through a field of flowers.

The rough canvas, the globs of dried pigment, the spatters of white—none of it registers in its merely material quality when the observer stands at the proper distance. All of these unpromising substances and clever tricks collaborate to help us objectify something largely contained *within our mind* but, for that very reason, imperceptibly locked away.

How would I recognize that my destiny lies in a higher dimension if I did not feel my wife, my son, my youth, and my energy slowly slipping from me every time I see more wrinkles in the mirror? How would I know (or divine) that the ultimate fusion of all dimensions holds beatitude if faint crosscurrents did not touch me with a thrill not of this world—with a joy inextricably woven into pain, since to feel the joy's access is to feel its egress? The happiest Christmas morning you'll ever spend with your child, when he is yet young enough to be caught up naively in the mystery of wrapped presents and bright bows, has tiny veins of grief running through it; for you know that the wrappers will be shredded, the bows tossed aside, the boxes opened, the tree's stand left bare, and tomorrow's dawn haunted by a unique emptiness. If you're at all thoughtful, you know every bit of this well before Christmas Eve.

The acutely wry final words of Giacomo Leopardi's "Sabato del Villaggio" just leapt into my head: *ma la tua festa / ch'anco tardi a venir non ti sia grave*—"but be not dismayed that your holiday seems slow in coming." For such as we are, anticipation colors much of the holy day's joy: the day itself is never a match for the hopes it inspires. Even so does the master painter's skill deceive his admirers with coarse fabric and smeared splotches. We know what we really want: something that we can't have—not while we remain in this world. Only we don't really know it... or our only chance of really knowing it, at any rate, is to wander through this world's art gallery—its long *linear* corridor of displays—until the exit door abandons us to scenes that are no longer enough.

What if the gallery's long corridor were itself a kind of canvas; what if, that is, we think of linear time as the medium upon which numinous flashes of experience are represented? Our default mode of conception is just the opposite. True time (we presume) runs along its straight-laid track from station to station as effect succeeds cause, and memorable moments pop up along the way like haphazard but picturesque cottages and meadows glimpsed through the train's windows. Reverse the polarities, though, and consider. What if our souls were immersed in this world, by agency of a delicate and decaying body, in order to amass a stock of transcendent encounters intended to teach mystery and reverence; and what if these encounters were arranged along a linear chronology that really had no ultimate purpose other than to provide background for the display? What if our human presumption, favoring the side of the arrangement that we more readily comprehend, were positioning us too close to the paintings, so that our attention was absorbed by the rough texture of canvas and dried pigment—not by the transformative magic of harmonized shades in soft light?

What if part of our initiation, indeed, were a kind of test to see if we could distinguish between the more accessible illusion which leaves our intelligence in greater control and the more evasive reality which rouses our spirit to greater activity? What if we were being set free in the gallery to figure out for ourselves the perspective of higher reward, just as I was once forced—in my untutored, blundering youth—to discover a few basic principles of painting on my own after stumbling upon several masterpieces?

Throughout this book, I have said much of memories. Specifically, I have placed a premium upon memory as the preservative of moments durably present throughout our spinning calendar-days. Would it be too bold at this point to suggest that our most indelible memories are the answer—indeed, the antidote—to our pitilessly aging bodies? I suppose most of us gravitate, whether by nature or culture, to some quasi-scientific notion of recollection as a series of favorite snapshots stored and "photo-shopped" in our neurons. The empirical evidence is sparse to non-existent for such casual explanations… but they dispel all mystery, which seems to satisfy the popular definition of science.   Especially in the case of pleasant occurrences (so the orthodoxy runs), we revisit images of the past until we wear a kind of rut; and the rut, furthermore, is sown with daffodils and cleansed of any smelly little carcasses along the way. Everybody knows about the gilding of nostalgia. That factor alone should induce us to discount the testimony of memory: it's an unreliable witness because of its drippy sentimentality.   It doesn't "lead to anything productive" when consulted uncritically. It simply distracts our concentration with happy faces and birthday balloons.

Such dismissive caricatures of what I have called crosscurrents strike me as having little correspondence to the truth. Yes, I've heard the conversations that "good old boys" have at reunions. This one over here ran in the winning touchdown on a fumble—remember that? That one over there blundered into an evening with the most beautiful girl on campus when the computer-dating thing was used to organize a dance—glitch in the software! (Laughs all around.) And who could forget the "study group" at Mitch's house when his parents were gone for the weekend? And so on, and so on....

Occasions like these are gold mines for sociologists who might wish to research how people adapt themselves to overworked and badly stretched narratives in order to signal their solidarity with a certain clique. They have nothing to do with an "out of time" moment.

Indeed, the three examples I summoned up randomly all just happen to involve some degree of delirium or inebriation that would—if and when the event truly occurred—have undermined concentration upon the moment.

As was clarified in the genuine examples I offered much earlier, the crosscurrent may well be a painful recollection, or at least possess some element of unsettling mystery or tragic poignancy. It's usually a rather (or very) private moment, too. And as a moment, it may be a mere fragment of an event, or a sensation of strange presence not integrated into any subsequent event.

Speaking of high school reunions (which I avoid like the plague), I can vividly recall certain lingering scenes from my own haggard adolescence on the campus in question. Most have no social quality at all—no encounter or exchange with another person. In fact, none of the very many pleasant and rewarding conversations with my college students much later on—and some of these are only a couple of years old—possesses a transcending, timeless quality: at no point in my life have the classrooms and corridors of any educational institution ever catalyzed a "standing above time" moment within me. Instead, when I recall such moments from high school, they tend to be settings in open spaces: panoramic views in mid-afternoon, after classes were out, that I would take in from the main building's exit or from a soccer field. Bright low sun, wide blue sky, wintry brown grass, raggedly undeveloped real estate spread before a distant line of woods... ironically peaceful settings. Perhaps the message in the chilly, unobstructed breeze was, "They know not what they do"... or perhaps it was more a reprise of the earlier warning from my treehouse experience: "The world is going to be far too vast for me ever to figure out." Some of both, no doubt.

In any case, those visions are razor-sharp. They're not well-worn passages. I don't lift them gently from a mental treasure chest every so often, unwrap them, and spread them on the table to admire. They come after years and years of neglect—and they come instantly focused, and... well, *present*. They are part of my eternal moment. In comparison to them, events and images from just a month ago may prove utterly irrecoverable. Why is that? Why does a minutely resolved snapshot slap me in the face as I prowl in a dark corner, but my trip into town last week has already melted into a thousand similar trips? What trump card has neurological science to play on this inexplicable phenomenon that will render it just another ho-hum, "your brain's fooling you" bit of routine?

I've noticed that patients suffering from Alzheimer's or some similar form of dementia will often retrieve extremely precise (and extremely accurate, as far as anyone can tell) scenes from childhood that they haven't thought about in decades. As my mother's mind deteriorated in her final months, such moments came flooding in upon her. I had never heard her mention any of them before, and she herself usually expressed amazement that they seemed to appear from nowhere and immediately became so clear. No, Professor Neurologist, I don't really think we understand what's happening here. Go ahead and call it a trick of misfiring neurons. As a theory, that explanation sits comfortably beyond proof or disproof... so let's just opt for the humdrum dismissal that keeps us pointed up the Tunnel of Scientific Progress. By all means!

But what if the collection of such moments, such fragments, is why we're here in this temporal valley of tears and shadows? What if we are being taught sorrow that we may one day understand joy—and what if that day is the Last Day, a dawn that no longer needs a dusk? What if this winding corridor of time that we try so hard to straighten out—that we transform into a cosmic vacuum cleaner, so that it sucks up everything we do in "progress"—was intended by our creator merely to be a backdrop, a blank canvas? And look at us! What fools we are, paying more attention to the canvas's rugged fibers than to how the Girl in the Scarf gazes at us!

Christ patiently explained to the scoffing Sadducees, who were far too "clever" to believe in life after death, that our soul's form in eternity is liberated from the corporeal properties weighing it down here and now. We will be like angels. I suppose we may actually have wings, of a sort! At least I don't have to worry about eventually losing my sight or my mind—or being able to eat almost nothing, or growing incontinent, or feeling pain in every joint. I'll take a pass on the wings if only I can live as free of those worries as I did half a century ago!

For now, however—for the temporal, temporary moment—we need these sad bodies. How else will we learn that we are not gods, but servants of God? Those who labor mightily toward the transformation of the body into a semi-robotic super-computer are fixated, precisely, on becoming God... and the only thing they seem to be accomplishing is the steady elimination of their humanity.

This black-and-white representation of J.M.W. Turner's *Glaucus and Scylla* is, of course, an abomination against one of the eternal masters of color and texture; but of texture, at least, we can divine a little something by looking closely. Especially as you study the fading sunlight's effects in the broad sky and over the placid sea (whose peace Scylla will transform once she completes her metamorphosis into a monster), notice the traces of bold brush strokes heavily laden with paint.

CHAPTER NINETEEN

The Paradox of Epochal Change

> "Two men went up into the temple to pray; the one a Pharisee, the other a
> publican. The Pharisee stood and prayed thus with himself, 'God, I thank
> thee, that I am not as other men are, extortioners, unjust, adulterers, or even
> as this publican. I fast twice in the week, I give tithes of all that I possess.'
> And the publican, standing afar off, would not lift up so much as his eyes
> unto heaven, but smote his breast, saying, 'God be merciful to me a sinner.'
> I tell you, this man went down to his house justified rather than the other:
> for every one that exalteth himself shall be abased; and he that humbleth
> himself shall be exalted."   Luke 18.10-14

**Believers are asked to accept that each individual soul is vitally important
to God and, if saved, abides with Him in eternity; yet when we confront
human history (and the much vaster sub-structure of pre-history), we see
no evidence that individual lives matter. The greatest monuments of
entire empires scarcely endure as rubble.**

We have already had frequent occasion to note that the plunge of
linear time into decline happens on a cosmic as well as an individual
level. Things have come and gone for ages of ages on earth—and not
just short-lived things like gnats or long-lived things like sea turtles, but
entire species; even entire eras with their bizarre troves of trilobites or
dinosaurs. We discussed how the Darwinian Revolution transformed
this prospect of vast futility into an ascending staircase... and not
necessarily as Charles Darwin would have liked. Our adoring worship
of the future, with its smug confidence in tomorrow's self-justifying
moral superiority, has—for at least a century—surely been the single
most exercised means of redeeming our paltry human lives from
insignificance.

For, of course, it's at the human level that time's enormity deals
the keenest blow to our religious faith. Dinosaurs can be a long
planetary nightmare without disturbing our personal sleep, but our own
futility on this earth is almost intolerable. A while back, I mentioned
Hamlet's grim musing as he held Yorick's skull. I mentioned François
Villon and the "snows of yesteryear". I might have mentioned, as well,

a couplet penned by the Roman poet Propertius on behalf of his ailing lover—lines which one of my professors (an utterly dissolute and directionless human being) rightly admired:

Sunt apud infernos tot milia formosarum;
Pulchra sit in superis, si licet, una locis.

There are so many thousands of beautiful women among the dead;
May but this one lovely girl bide with the living a while!

All of these poets underscore the same point: it's not just our own aging and eventual death with which we must come to terms. Indeed, our self-centered fear of annihilation almost disappears as we contemplate that of every extraordinary person around us. All human beings must endure the same sad decline, except for those cut off tragically (or mercifully?) in their prime; and such has been the fate of our kind for as long as its members have walked the earth. The chronological sublime? Yes, there's a sort of transcendent melancholy that can petition God's throne as we stroll through a vast graveyard. Sometimes, however, we just want to sit by the freshest mound and waste away—or hurl ourselves in a gaping hole "full of snails," writes Baudelaire, "where I can at my leisure hide my bones from sun / and, as a shark cuts waves, drift through oblivion."

Frankly, our progenitors have been trying to reverse the polarities of Creation's apparently downward spiral for quite some while. Long before Darwin proposed that the fittest were sowing their superior seed through the future, hints were floated that—just maybe—the cream was rising to the top. Karl Popper believed that Heraclitus (soon to be imitated by Plato) was the first in Western tradition to "historicize" our cycle of life and death into a struggle of superior men against a chaotic rabble. Hesiod's Golden Age (referred to in the last chapter) was stood on its ear. Heroes... they were still coming! Be patient! Rome's great epic poet Virgil represents the unborn generations queued up in the Underworld as the secret to his race's predestined world-dominance. Indeed, his poem's overhaul of the *Odyssey*'s Hades—now a kind of locker room where the A-team waits to take the field—was to become a commonplace in European epic for the next sixteen hundred years. How we all wanted King Arthur to be rowed back to our shore from his otherworldly Avalon!

Between you and me, just because Virgil was paid by political propagandists doesn't mean that he hadn't seen through the lust for power. I'm convinced that, on the contrary, he had little confidence in the future's holding any possible earthbound utopia. His *Aeneid* portrayed all too clearly (except to the dim eyes of his paymasters) the misery that man's grand schemes bring upon him and his dependents in the present... and portrayed, too—with a clarity that had much of the Old Testament about it—the persistence of this hard lesson throughout the ancient past.

But Virgil, you know, at last fell prey to severe depression. Suetonius claims that he left instructions for the *Aeneid*—an unfinished masterpiece that he had been more than a decade composing—to be burned after his death. Too much honesty in admitting the Golden Age's demise crushes us humans. We even tinkered with the clock's hands so as to hasten the "end time" promised by Christ! Our culture began its two Christian millennia by struggling to break out of the life-and-death cycle immediately. It embraced an apocalyptic kind of faith: God was bringing history to an abrupt end very soon—be ready! (We study the enigma of Christ's "end is near" pronouncement in the next chapter.) Then, when the end hadn't come as the first millennium wound down, we sought a deeper sense of purpose in the arts, and in a nurture of individualism that benefited the arts. There is a sort of immortality, after all, in beautiful creations. The turn to more secular escapes in a sequence of renaissances (including the one with an upper-case "r") also favored, alas, a turn to more secular ambitions... and the rest, so sayeth the cliché, is history. The Old Testament's cycle of self-destructive worldly aspirations, so powerfully reproduced Virgil, closed its curve without anyone's paying much attention.

I could blandly assert here, "That's where we are today." But it isn't. We're in a worse place. As a student of history (linear chronology and all), I am unaware of ever having seen evidence that a society has sunk quite as low as we have. For our resistance to the apparent futility of life on earth hasn't just goaded us into adoring a gilded tomorrow: it has now lured us, very recently, into defaming the past. Epic poets needed precedent to provide context for their vision of an elevated future. Evolutionary scientists need the past to provide stable building blocks for the ascending staircase of superior survival rates. Our contemporary intellectuals, and only they (as far as I know), have hit upon the trick of generating an illusory ascent simply by hurling everything behind them into the pit. The lazy man's substitute for a ladder: stay where you are and strike down everything around you. Our ancestors, we're lectured, were rapist cavemen who subjugated women more savagely than lions tear apart hyenas. Our more immediate forebears were racist slavemasters whose every accomplishment reeks of their human chattel's blood and sweat. Why, we have only to stand where we are and draw a breath to be immeasurably superior to the scum that sired us!

If human life in fact has worth, and if the prospect of linear history presents a crushing futility that casts any such abiding worth into question, then the current Ivory Tower strategy of solving the paradox is an appallingly shortsighted answer; for how will our children's lives, in turn, find any worth except by consigning our lives, as well, to the Spittoon of the Past? Perhaps the answer to why our intellectuals want no children and, indeed, want the human race to go sterile lies herein: perhaps they're jealous of their position as the Last Man Standing.

Yet such a position isn't merely inane. From the perspective of the Eternal Moment, it is loathsome—it is profoundly despicable. For if our higher mission in traveling history's linear road is to get off the road—to absorb as many moments as we can of full being rather than chasing what we don't have in dimensions where we'll never get it— then our predecessors are actually our companions. Our fathers and grandfathers are our brothers. We know of the external events, from beginning to end, that their earthly time spanned, while they knew little or nothing of our day's headlines; and, naturally, we don't know what ordeals may face our children and grandchildren. In that sense, the timeline is inviolable.

But we know what an ordeal is (or we'll certainly find out, at any rate). Morally—spiritually—our great-great-grandfathers are as "now" as we. They, too, struggled when young to make sense of parental love in the context of parental authority. They, too, came of age and sought to found their own families, to stabilize their own positions in the world. They, too, reluctantly made the acquaintance of illness, decline, and death. They walk, not at our back, but at our side. And Virgil walks there, too—and Saul called Paul, and Moses, and Abraham.

Indeed, if such a thing as prophecy exists, it must surely do so as a result of the inspiration provided by moral insight. I can imagine without much strain that a deeply spiritual person, aware far beyond the average of what starlight and what hellfire compete to ignite the human heart, might foresee coming events with great accuracy. To my mind, Virgil did this (if his *Aeneid* is read at a deeper level than Classics departments teach it). Other great authors have done it, as well. I know that Jordan Peterson would nominate Nietzsche and Dostoyevsky, though I personally could wish that their style were a little less "crazy"... but then, prophets are supposed to sound crazy, aren't they?

If only we can picture human existence in this biaxial manner—our flesh-and-blood generations falling one into another like dominoes, our spiritual beings compressed into a common and ever-present struggle—then the passive despair of the interminable line disappears in the active drama of good battling evil. Not just particular generations, but particular individuals acquire a significance that can't be ignored. Those bodies that lie moldering in the enormous cemetery possessed souls whose life is right here, right now... right among us. We are not plankton floating in the turgid, boundless ocean—and we needn't be Baudelaire's shark riding comatosely in a wave. All of us who have ever lived, rather, are comrades engaged in the fight against "graveyard oblivion". Our bodies, living in earthly chronology, tell us that resistance is futile. Our souls tell us that the world is trying to warp our perspective yet again.

When those of our contemporaries who spit upon the past ascribe all the vilest motives they can find in their hearts to previous generations, therefore, they are undermining some of the firmest spiritual ground in our temporal lives. They would divorce us—or themselves, and whoever is fool enough to follow them—irreconcilably from our own kind, our brothers and sisters who happened to live sooner. Slander of a human being whose soul has passed from his body is no less vicious than slander of the man in the next room. A wicked tongue is not less wicked, but more so, if it unleashes its arrogant condescension upon those no longer present to defend themselves. Of course, all are present in the Eternal Present; and I doubt, for that matter, that our long-deceased brethren would volunteer much in their defense. They failed innumerable times as we fail every day. Yet anyone who deplores their failures as if they belonged to a lesser species adds to his own balance of sin a new failure unknown to most of them.

Why would our creator put us in such a complex position, where we must tax our imagination not just to accept the worth of every individual ever to draw breath, but also to accept that our predecessors are really our forever-contemporaries? Maybe one reason is precisely to put us to the test: to let us prove our worth against this vice of thrusting our ancestors beneath the soles of our grinding shoes. For what honest, generous heart would not abstain from such behavior even without higher inspiration? Who is not naturally disposed to remember his grandparents with respect? To be sure, loving respect cannot by itself redeem us from despair—but surely it conditions the good heart to look further for a message of hope.

On the other hand, those of us who prefer to condemn the apparent past have condemned themselves in exploiting past ambiguities to "occupy the high ground". They have left no room for the spirit to touch them: they have already staked out the clouds as their own proper realm. Creation's design, I suspect, conceals many such examples of our being set free to serve as our own judge and jury. Receive judgment from thine own mouth, thou who wouldst judge!

CHAPTER TWENTY

The Paradox of Time's Fulfillment

"For the Son of Man shall come in the glory of his Father with his angels;
and then he shall reward every man according to his works. Verily I say
unto you, there be some standing here which shall not taste of death, till
they see the Son of Man coming in his kingdom."
Matthew 16.27-28

**The believer is asked to accept that secular time is moving in linear
fashion toward completion, when every purpose for which God created
the world will have been accomplished. Yet the idea of incompletion does
not suit God's self-sufficiency, on the one hand—while, on the other, it
implies that His human servants should be advancing some cause or
causes within historical time rather than seeking spiritual serenity.**

Like the previous one, this final paradox typically strikes people as
a macrocosmic rather than a microcosmic puzzle. My first two
paradoxes were conceived against the draining sand of a single
lifetime's hour-glass. To wit: our personal "rebirth" during whatever
few years we live seems incoherent from many angles. Then, if we
ponder the insertion of our glorious soul into an ever-weak and soon-
declining body, we encounter more apparent contradiction. Paradox
Three sought to represent the individual upon the vastly broader screen
of history's totality—a perspective that makes our struggle to find
meaning as minuscule units seem laughable against the gaping, often
futile span of human endeavor on earth. Ingeniously but ruinously, we
have sometimes tried to wrench that sweeping plain upward until it
resembles a steady progress capable of turning our tiny corpses to
stepping stones. Our species insists during such historical phases that
humanity is getting better and better as, from their massed numbers, its
members squint at a shifting future from wobbly tiptoes.

Well... isn't that just what Christianity tells us we should do: get
better? In fact, as a "worldview", doesn't Christianity promote a linear
outlook? As a fairly young college professor, I recall thinking myself
pretty clever when I happened upon a way of representing the change

from oral-traditional, tribal cultures steeped in myth (like Homer's Greece) to more literate, progress-minded cultures (like the post-Socratic Greek world). Oral societies, as I noted early in this book, think of earthly events as occurring in cycles. "What has been is what will be; there's nothing new under the sun," sayeth the Preacher. As these same societies grow more literate and tech-savvy, however, they become aware that external circumstances could be somewhat manipulated. Life could be made more tolerable: the crueler cycles could be broken.

The new Christian faith erupted in this Mediterranean world of transformation spreading under Roman rule. In Christ, we see an agency who will shatter for us the grinding treadmill of sin. Tomorrow can now be different from yesterday, for the believer. Not only that... but the entirety of human history is no longer slavishly turning the same old pointless wheel. A clock has been set ticking. Christ will return. History as we know it will end. Those who have refused to assume a gentle yoke and engage a mild ascent will be judged and cast out, while those who have accepted the light burden of a higher destiny will inherit the kingdom of heaven.

Circles and lines covered my blackboard—or not lines, exactly, but ascending curves. As I say, I thought I was very clever.

And, to be sure, I hadn't utterly missed the boat. Christ does confide to his apostles (in the verses at this chapter's banner) that some of their generation will not taste death before the Second Coming. Naturally, the apostles interpreted this to mean that the world beneath their feet must end within three or four decades, at most. Or if not all them so interpreted his words, then several succeeding generations of believers surely did. The early church had a distinctly, disturbingly millenarian tinge. Groups of Christians prepared for the Rapture in a fashion that we instantly associate today with cultism. Some of their practices were vaguely suicidal, as if they wished to speed up the process lest the Lord's utterance be proved false. I was reminded just the other day by a radio commentator's remarks that a certain segment of American Christendom wants to help Israel, not out of political loyalty or common humanity, but because a devastating Israeli conflict is said in the Book of Revelation to precede the Second Coming.

So now we face two problems. First, as an older and (I hope) much wiser man, I recognize that my upward-curving schematic of the future according to Christianity turns our faith into a progressivist delivery system. Christians, it seems, are actually intended to be gazing at the far horizon as they stumble into pothole after pothole on today's road. Our duty, apparently, is to ignore present obstacles and attend only to a gilded vision on a hilltop. This is the very delirium that I have consistently identified in the preceding pages as sabotaging genuine faith! I've known ministers, indeed, who enthusiastically embraced the naïveté (and even the stupidity) of certain charitable or missionary undertakings because... because we're supposed to be the Lord's fools in this world. Are they right?

Of course, the other problem is that the futuristic emphasis robs my numinous moments—my crosscurrents—of any real value. My case on their behalf makes me just another lunatic... or a rarer sort of lunatic, perhaps: one who sees magic in the present rather than projecting it ever farther into the future (that road down which so many cans are kicked). If our calling as Christians is truly to immerse ourselves in inept behavior having no relation to present realities as we prepare for a transport beam, then everything I have come to believe in my heart and mind is falsehood.

On the other hand, Christ's words do appear to promise an imminent return, do they not? And that return certainly didn't occur within a generation, or even two or three, did it? And that would make his words, as recorded, a falsehood... would it not?

No, not necessarily... not if my older, wiser heart has steered me true. For, in that case, all of us humans who have ever lived are but one generation: our bodies die and decay in the ground, wave after wave after wave—but the time of our spirits is a contemporaneity of superimposed layers. Spiritually, we are all living in the same day. Before that single day ends, some of us will have turned our attention to the light's true source... and some of us will be rushing toward a dark valley's ingenious array of manmade beacons. So it has always been—except that, after Christ, the warning against the valley's artificial necklaces and jewels removes every good excuse for error.

I concluded the previous chapter by conjecturing that the superior appeal of linear time to our limited human intelligence may be a kind of test—a trap, even, whose success or failure at catching us is a judgment we pass upon ourselves; for if our "rebirth" is genuine, the snare doesn't close. May the seduction of this progressive, millenarian timeline not also be a setting for self-judgment? For if you would drink poison or starve yourself to death in order to bring God's kingdom to earth, then you don't know the way; if you would invite a catastrophic international war for the same purpose, then you don't know the way; if you would shower strangers with gifts just because of how they dress or speak, never concerning yourself with their real needs or with the presence of cutthroat thieves among them, then you don't know the way; if you would live today as if it were tomorrow, looking straight through this morning's sunlight to adore a brighter sun in your imagination, then you have lost your way.

Christ's promise has a thirty-to-forty-year shelf-life for those who hear it with the ears of this world. It rings false to those who speak a degenerate language. Its truth is perceptible only to those who understand that one moment in this world's linear time can outlast the entire spectrum of years we have on earth, encompassing the whole because it floats free of the whole. Yes, the promise offers an ascent... but the ascent is right here, right now. You don't progress to that height by clambering over heaps of unobserved, ignored refuse at your feet: you thrust your head into it by standing firm on the ground beneath you.

I know this to be true, because I find goodness in standing firm rather than pretending to walk on a cloud; and I know it to be true, because I have seen—over and over, in myself and others—the culpable folly of ignoring the present to dwell in a fantasy.

I initially labeled this chapter an answer to a macrocosmic paradox. Nevertheless, I recognize that my answer has significant implications for one of faith's most intimate struggles. I am no longer young; I am, indeed, departing middle age. I think more and more about death. How exactly do we get from the body to the place where our soul was always meant to be? Is that, too, a staircase—another ascending line? People who have endured Near-Death Experiences even describe it, frequently, as a tunnel!

But perhaps, once again, our material conditioning is corrupting our powers of conception. Perhaps the other world—full, true reality— is right here, right now. It's all around us, just as the Last Day is this day we now live... only we can't understand how that might be so. Trying to explain my notion to someone recently, I suggested that we live this life in a great bag—a bag plenty big enough to allow us to move around, and hence fully able to deceive us about how tightly it constricts our view. Its interior is adorned with various scenes that keep us occupied or amused; and enough light penetrates from numerous holes in our sack's fabric that we have little difficulty distinguishing the artificial events coated in glitter. When we die, however, the bag is wholly stripped from us... and we find that the light entering through those pinprick holes was in fact our only reliable evidence of genuine reality. Now it floods us round about, and its source is as deep as a galaxy's cradle; but when we yet endured the suffocation in that sack which we naively called life, we treated the pricks of light as mere conveniences to assist us in admiring our prison's walls. On our quest after ultimate meaning, we expected finally to walk into one of those glistening murals that represented a virgin forest or a great city. We never suspected that the whole thing was a fragile show and that the truth was at our shoulder—a slender, steady, faithful thread of perfect light.

And—to finish in the macrocosmic once more—as your or my particular death shall be liberation from a shroud, so the "completion" of God's creation is already accomplished in its apparent stages of becoming. God does not require a timeline (after the fashion of one of our tunnels) to work the kinks out of His universe. Rather, that living moment which seems motion through time to us is the job already done. Something tells me that even after the body's death, the soul will find much in need of its attention: relatives and acquaintances to be visited, great souls of the distant past (that is, the more obscured present) to be met, questions to be asked and answered, pardons to be requested and accepted... so very much work will await us. The labor of infinite joy! Yet all of that is already happening, right now, and has indeed always been happening. It was all implied in every one of those strange moments which left us spellbound for a worldly instant before we got on with our "useful" business.

Concluding Remarks

seeking God's presence is not "New Age mysticism"

It's an awkward task for a book that wanders among the matters of heaven and earth as much as this one has done to attempt any sort of summary or farewell. Nevertheless, I'm going to address with all possible brevity three questions that I may somewhat clumsily have left lingering in the air (along with a lot of unsettled dust).

Is this a book of "New Age mysticism"? Am I offering some preposterously subjective concoction of self-help and wishful thinking of the sort that litters lists of recent publications and bends the shelves at Barnes and Noble?

If I were indeed seeking to be the hour's latest guru, I would have been greatly assisted by having starred in a couple of movies or a Netflix serial, or at least having played in a Super Bowl or anchored a news desk—or, at the very least, having been born with the same name as a celebrity of that sort. But I'm a nobody with a "nobody" kind of name (almost as abundant, wherever names are enrolled, as "Joe Smith"). My ruminations about God and the spirit must stand on their own feet. My autograph will draw no attention to them.

What I can offer is what any human being can always offer: an appeal to the human head and heart. To the basic good sense dwelling within most of my fellow creatures, I would say that we are a miserable race—born to misery and doomed to misery, as long as we have none but earthly resources. We are naturally inclined to seek pleasure; but the most obvious, bluntest pleasures import numerous, often enormous problems into our lives. Our rawest joys are usually obtained at someone else's expense, and they may also—around the edges—be impeded by laws targeting riotous conduct. They're expensive, as well, to both body and pocketbook. They're by no means easily accessed all of the time. And worst of all, they evaporate almost as soon as they reach their height. Tonight's orgy is soon tomorrow's stinking room of overturned furniture and kitchen counters become roach havens. It's hard for any intelligent being to justify life at such a level.

So we devote ourselves to acquiring wealth—which we had already done, to some extent, because parties must be paid for... but now we apply our efforts to the chore with a vengeance. We will party with more discretion and refinement. We'll drink wine instead of beer. We'll collect a trophy wife instead of taking potluck at the local tavern, and we'll live in the best section of town (where maids come in to erase the evidence of the "morning after"). We'll tap into a wholly new and more rarified type of pleasure, as well: respectability. "I am become a name," says Tennyson's Ulysses; yes, we'll become "a name". Join a church, be an alderman... maybe run for political office at some point. People will approach us humbly for favors. Our soirées will be designed to keep invitees to an exclusive minimum rather than challenged to scrounge up enough footloose cronies for a Friday-night debauch.

Yet that more distinguished destination, too, soon begins to seem fatally stalled in obscurity if we do nothing to thrust it forward. So from wealth and fame we mix the yet rarer martini of power. Running for public office, yes: that's the ticket. "Your man! Your kind of man! Speaks for your values! He listens to you from his 5,000-square-foot house and successful law firm! His beautiful wife and daughters are just like yours—he's just a family man!" Power. Power can teach an upside-down kind of humility, once we get it. So much ability to affect so many lives... well, now, what should we actually do with all this thunder?

Make some noise with it—make a difference! Make life better for everyone! People are so miserable, you know... and now we have power over them. So we begin to do for them the things that they're too foolish (in their endless morning-afters and their ignorance of games within games) to do for themselves. We become their messiah. We organize their time for them, regulate their spending and behavior, minutely moderate the conditioning to which their children are submitted in schools (lest they grow to be the same fools as their parents). We play God. We have the thunderbolt, and so we throw it.

Sometimes, in our little bit of humility, we consent merely to be God's right hand rather than God Almighty. Perhaps the most arrogant, power-consumed persons I have ever known personally conceive of themselves as the Lord's humble servants. With a sweep of their pastoral palm (and I'm not implying that they are *pastors*— only that they regard others as sheep), they wave vast segments of humanity into this pen over here because of a shared skin color and language. The troughs are filled to the brim, and every little lamb is given an antiseptic dip. Other flocks are chuted into the slaughterhouse for being uncooperative, or simply for having fed too well the previous week. God's humble servant understands the principles of separation: the rest of us, to whom high knowledge has not been revealed, must simply have faith that love is at work.

I don't know that the person who grows addicted to power rather than merely drunk on it ever sobers up. His or her abiding misery can always be addressed through the hocus-pocus of one more massive reform, one more purge, one more Five Year Plan. Or if the moment of truth, of facing up to utter futility, does indeed arrive, it probably finds our holy warrior on his deathbed. Stalin's daughter apparently observed him shaking his fist at heaven with his final breath.

For the rest of us, drunkenness on life's lesser intoxicants is more likely to allow a kind of hung-over clairvoyance wherein the folly of our ways stands starkly naked. I don't see how—I *cannot* see how—a recommendation to stop chasing neon lights into the night is far-out pseudo-spirituality. To me, it looks like the commonest of common sense. My appeal, therefore, has been to every person's natural-born reason, inasmuch as reason can find nothing within our tight terrestrial box capable of liberating us. A rational human being will be forced, sooner or later, to admit a) that life is insanely, invincibly irrational, or b) that the purpose of life cannot be accomplished by living within the comprehensible terms of life. That's your ultimately reasonable choice, thou Enlightened Man of our time: either go hang yourself and stop posing a menace to others, or realize that you were not made for ends fully within your understanding.

Now, that I should have positioned the windows upon higher realization right in front of us—right here, right now—must surely be the harder part of my presentation to choke down. For all immediate windows seem to open upon futility: that's the problem—that's why we chase neon lights, gilded horizons, and swirling galaxies (with black holes at their center). The view from the window isn't often very inspiring. I confessed many pages ago to having willfully closed one such window myself. I no longer listen to music as I once did, simply because the contrast between those indivisible, free-floating moments of perfect beauty with the squalor of daily life drove me almost to despair. Yet that window wasn't really ever closed, because my memory could always play back Debussy or "the divine Perotin" or Giorgia Fumanti's rendition of "Espiritu" any time it liked.

And isn't that more often the truth about all the ugliness around us? It's not that we cannot find uplifting, irrepressibly *present* moments through many a window on any given day: it's that such moments would distract us too much from the unsavory task at hand. The world as it truly is—i.e., as God's creation—rustles constantly with crosscurrents; the world as we have made it, always trying to make it "better", is a dark tunnel whose every remunerative chore involves sealing more holes and crevices.

If, all smug and tough and "realist", you think that beauty doesn't exist or that stopping to watch a sunrise is half a step from legalizing hallucinogens, then continue on with your "rational" endeavor of amputating the rational mind's non-quantitative half. Your software upgrade will be awaiting you in the near future, primed by an injection of nanobots. (An all-synthetic cerebral transformation, I suppose, doesn't qualify as hallucinogenesis... though why shouldn't it?)

concentrating upon present realities is not "politicizing faith"

Another protest occurs to me—one which the paragraphs just above may have resuscitated: "What you call spirituality is far too political. You don't name names, but you virtually condemn entire initiatives and platforms in the current political arena. That doesn't sound very spiritual at all!"

We appear to be very sensitive these days to how things "look" or "sound". I suppose it could be a by-product of living our lives on screens—lives where we ourselves are increasingly actors projected before our own eyes. I don't really care about the "sound". The *truth* here is that politics has been hunting on forbidden preserves, not I. Political ideology has usurped the role of faith—and, indeed, it has invaded and occupied the religious space in our existence with all the ruthless tyranny of a cult. A healthily functioning political system should secure for its citizens the freedom to seek God in their own fashion, as long as they do not obstruct their neighbor's search in the process. If you have young children in a public school or run a small business that services weddings, tell me how comfortable you are these days with government's respect for your freedom of worship!

To be sure, free practice of one's faith generally includes being permitted to raise one's children within that faith; and, just as surely, we citizens of "multicultural" societies are apt to find ourselves nowadays in a thicket of briars where followers of certain creeds condition their children to torment believers of other persuasions. Whenever you blunder into a briar patch, you should move very slowly, extricating yourself from snags even as you try to avoid waiting thorns. You don't barge your way through—not without leaving a trail of blood behind.

The reigning political ideology of our time, however, tackles the briar patch like a bull elephant in rut. It handles cultism (the variety of religion that tutors young people to become bigots) by transforming itself into the Cult of Cults. All must obey the political *Supremo*. Any faith that bends a knee to the State's Elected and Anointed One may qualify as a subsidiary cult (and may well profit handsomely from that designation). In return (and for the time being), the State will prop up said cult by punishing its critics, who are also likely to be critics of arbitrary state power.

A rather fine collaboration can indeed be orchestrated between the Cult and her fledgling cults. (The image of Spenser's hideous Errour and the loathsome offspring who feed on her entrails keeps pestering me.) Consider the thick layers of moralism that now suffocate our political life. Charity is defined by the State in tax codes, and strict compliance is enforced by stiff penalties that include jail time. Persecution is defined by the State through its hierarchy of "protected classes", and the stiff-necked who treat all people equally are hounded into bankruptcy. Blasphemy is defined by the State in such edicts as "speech codes", and psychic priests known as public prosecutors pursue malefactors with "hate crime" statutes. Adoration is inculcated by the State through its "educational" institutions, and disrespect of approved saints and prophets is negatively reinforced by assigning low grades (with consequent damage to the sacrilegious student's employment prospects).

I don't want to belabor the point here. Yet part of the reason I sensed a certain obligation to address it at all is that young people in my immediate family who are coming alive to religious faith display— in exact proportion to their awakening—an aversion to political subjects. I am, indeed, all but compelled to avoid any political allusion in a few of these relationships if I don't want people about whom I deeply care to slink away. Now, why is that? Why should newly ignited religious fervor stifle, as it grows, all objections to how politicians engineer our existence? Am I not actively witnessing in my own family the effects of progressivist programming—the knee-jerk yielding to legislators, I mean, as proper arbiters in matters of religious faith? The space in which a believer may permissibly practice his belief is ever narrower. I suppose one might gather oneself in a quiet corner and say "omm" without fear of giving offense... but even utter quietism eventually proved unsatisfactory to Stalin and Mao, who suspected that resignation to their worldly lunacy detracted from enthusiastic participation. And, after all, they were correct in that suspicion.

An integral part of seeing what God has given you this day—the sunrise, the wind in the trees, the soft rain against the window—is *refusing* to have your senses and your mind constantly redirected to an invisible horizon officially, extrinsically supplied to your imagination. You can't live in the "optimism" conceived by a tyrant's feverish, overreaching brain and also live in the reality created by God for your mind and body. No man can serve two masters.

imagining non-linear time is not "science-hatred"

But how can I keep harping on reality while also calling into question the hard reality of linear time? This is the final question which I can well understand a perplexed reader wanting to pose.

I won't reprise my discussion of the antinomies that undermine our "hard reality" of cause-and-effect, falling-domino time. Enough (I hope) to repeat that this reality is far less "hard" than it is habitual. It's a gift from God, to be sure, such linear thinking: it is a fairly coherent manner (at least on an earthly scale) of assembling our perceptions. We think of time in lines because we *must* do so, given the limits of our human mentality. In the same way, we cannot picture a four-dimensional cone or sphere with any degree of sensual clarity, though mathematicians and physicists can perform complex operations using such geometry. We can recognize the possibility of a reality in other or additional dimensions, that is, but we can't directly perceive that reality.

My objective has been to perform the simplest of operations within a blueprint of time that none of us can directly perceive. I grant that there can be no justification for my temporal tinkering if it represents a mere surge of whimsy... but it doesn't. On the contrary, we need to suppose that time is other, or more, than a flat, straight line if the *affective, non-empirical* reality of our life's most powerful sentiments—our appreciation of beauty, our admiration of self-surpassing nobility, and so forth—is to have any grounding. I will risk overemphasis if I repeat that forcing ourselves to live within the box of what we fully understand is forcing ourselves to be less than human. Yet maybe that point cannot be overemphasized.

For those who always insist on holding out for "scientific evidence", I might observe in passing that theoretical physics has been messing about for years now with such conceptions as parallel universes. Feel free to research "string theory"—and to attempt explaining it to me, if you enjoy exercises in futility. Yes, perhaps "worm holes" exist. Perhaps time, in the near future (as we imagine the future, farther down the road), will be demonstrated empirically to be multi-dimensional in ways that we can't visually picture. Or maybe it won't. I don't like making a spiritual proposition such as mine about "crosscurrents" dependent upon what trend may or may not sweep through Ivy League departments of Physics next year.

I do assure you that I am a great admirer of science. I just wish that it were a bit more aware of its kinship to poetry. A scientific theory, frankly, is little more than a metaphor that—for the time being—manifests numerous points of correspondence with directly perceived reality. Later on, as direct perception probes farther and farther beyond what the naked eye and naked ear can detect, these correspondences seem less numerous and impressive. Then some physicist-poet thinks of a better metaphor with additional points of match... and a new theory is off and running.

I'm all for perceiving things more closely. Just notice, would you, that the White Stag always slips away as soon as you reach out to grab a horn. Science will not end this chase. The truth that we hope—that we yearn—to seize at last must forever rest just beyond our best lens's power of resolution.

CONTACT THE AUTHOR

My personal email address—semperluxmundi@yahoo.com—draws its unwieldy length from my website of the same name: www.semperluxmundi.org. (The Latin means "always the light of the world"; *luxmundi* was not available, so I added the "always" part). The site actually has links to dozens of YouTube videos on subjects related to those discussed in *The Eternal Moment*. In fact, my attempts to handle such difficult topics before a camera often prodded me into further thoughts that eventually found their way to these pages.

Of course, I may also be reached via my Amazon Authors page: https://www.amazon.com/John-Harris/e/B077M39H9N/ref=dp_byline_cont_ebooks_1. A great many of my publications are anthologies of material gathered from work published during the two-decade lifespan of *Praesidium*, the quarterly journal of the now-defunct Center for Literate Values (no longer accessible online). A few volumes are completely overhauled editions of matter that I published independently several years ago; and still fewer have been created from scratch since my retirement. Many of these last have to do with century-old techniques of hitting a baseball, which has become perhaps my most consuming hobby!

I appreciate sincere, thoughtful responses of all sorts. I answer as quickly and as thoroughly as I possibly can.